365 DAYS PAST THE TRAFFIC LIGHTS

ROSE YAVNEH TAYLOR

PREFACE

How do you cope with the death of a parent at 24? The time when you're somewhere between independence and reliance on parents, figuring out who you are and what you want to do, trying to create and maintain friendships and a social life when your world is crumbling around you and no one understands. My memoir explores the moment of diagnosis, mapping treatments and the experience of becoming a carer for a parent, putting my life on hold and becoming immersed in medical settings, and then the aftermath of events following my father's passing.

The book predominantly spans one year, from the day of dad's death to the one-year anniversary, taking the reader between London, Atlanta, and Los Angeles.

I am an expert in my own grief. I knew I needed to produce a book that would be exactly what I wish I had been presented with the day my father died to use as an emotional guide. To know I wasn't going crazy, my emotions were 'normal', and how to handle life as a mid-20-something who had to suddenly mature and become independent whilst dealing with the loneliness that comes with experiencing grief at this age (and younger), trying to negotiate who you are and your life going forward.

ACKNOWLEDGMENTS

Along the lines of the proverb 'it takes a village' this has certainly been the case for me. My sincerest thanks:

To my mother and brother, and to my family, way too many to name individually but spanning the UK, Los Angeles and New York and the States in between, everyone has helped keep my mum, my brother and myself buoyant; to 'keep flying'. Special shout-out to my cousins, Hannah, Luke and Madeleine in London, who were always there for me and gave me the privilege of watching Madeleine grow from one to two and all the fun that came between.

To my boyfriend Ruaridh, for always finding something supportive to say at 2pm, 2am, 10pm, 6am, any time of day or night I needed you. For always being there in person or on FaceTime. I don't know how I would have really functioned this year without you. Thank you for all the tea, toast platters, carbonaras, roast dinners, putting up with probably an unhealthy amount of lavender pillow spray, supplying me with distractions from my grief as well as listening to my trauma and engaging in difficult conversations about it. The biggest cheerleader of my successes and up days, and the best comfort for all the down days. You were my rock to cling onto during the tsunami.

To Louisa, I couldn't have asked for a more supportive, kind, funny and attentive best friend. Thank you for spending practically every two minutes of your life messaging me and for never letting me lose my appetite during this time.

To this particular set of friends: Cezaria, Ffion, Shoshana, Sarah, Gemma, Lizzy, Liv, Gemma-Paige, Chris, Andy, Eddie, Curtis, Sam, Beatrice, Rachel, Alex. From the continuous messaging, flowers, dinners, visits, phone calls, prayers, recommendations, tissues, wine, each person has helped and supported me in different ways and at different times, and together have formed the weaves of the comfort blanket I so desperately needed. You all know what you've done for me.

To family friends who have consistently checked up on me, made containers of chicken noodle soup, reminded me what dad would have said at certain times, housed me or invited me to stay and made sure I was keeping afloat.

To my PhD supervisor who offered unwavering support both personal and academic during this time to help me stay on track. To my colleagues at my part time job who have been incredibly kind and understanding throughout. Lastly but in no means least, to Charlotte from Cruse Bereavement Care who listened to my ramblings and snotty sobs, helped to make things a little clearer and without whom I dread to think where my mental health would be.

TABLE OF CONTENTS

INTRODUCTION

Grieving is not a linear process, you don't get from A to B, you go round and round in circles, or sometimes tight frustrating coils, and sometimes longer, less frequent or intense spirals. You don't check an emotion off a list once you've felt it and then pass through opening gates to the next, it's a process of revolving doors, and coming to terms with that is hard but necessary.

I was 24 years, five months and 24 days old when my father died, still a student and dependent on him in many ways - financially, mentally and socially. I did not have my own children to focus my attention on, to hug at night or to keep my spirits up, although this is not to say that any age group is hit harder by losing a parent, after all everyone's family relationships are different.

As a PhD candidate studying Anthropology I wouldn't dream of writing anything without first endlessly reading relevant and wider literature, conducting in-depth research, and referencing works. How could I not? I'm not an expert in those topics, but I am an expert in my bereavement, in my feelings, and how I've managed to live my life for the first 365 days that followed losing dad.

After he passed away I began to document how I felt in order to aid my mental healing process. By writing a sentence or even one word down helped me 'empty' my head which for nearly a year felt completely full with thoughts and memories of trauma. Whilst writing my feelings down I realised that many more people, of either a similar age, or at a similar stage of life to myself, may be feeling the same, and if my words could offer insight or comfort to another, then that can only be positive and something my dad would be proud of. In truth, I wish I had been handed this book as the nurses shepherded us out of the hospital room following dad's passing.

When my father died I found very few resources connected with me; there were many meet-ups or group sessions for bereaved spouses, and many books about bereavement written by therapists or medical professionals which felt too cold and distant, and many about losing a parent penned by people who were much older and at very different stages of their lives to me, and most with their own nuclear family to care for.

As a result, I read them with a sense of bitterness and the urge to get my own feelings down on paper, to get *my* side of the story out. I almost felt territorial over emotions and reading other people experiencing them felt wrong or unfair. At that stage it didn't offer me comfort, but looking back I think I was scared to get hurt by what I may read, by knowing what may lie ahead of me in my healing process, written by people who I could not resonate with.

Through writing this I have really explored my emotions, put into words how I had been feeling, and attitudes towards things that had for so long only lived in my mind, accompanying me through my day and replaying at night as soon as my head touched a pillow.

There are, however, rawer moments and darker times that occurred behind closed doors not confessed in this book, some things are too personal to publicise yet I mention them vaguely here as they likely occur for many other people too.

This book is personal, but not private, I don't want it to be triggering or voyeuristic. Family dynamics are also impacted if people's grief is embodied and enacted in different ways, which often leads to a clash. I didn't speak to my twin brother for over a year.

Another major issue is the financial turmoil families are often left in after a death. Whether it's adapting to living on a one-person income, having to move house, sell cars, dealing with financial pressures left behind, learning how to deal with financial actions that were perhaps solely the deceased's responsibilities, or crippling medical and healthcare bills, (especially in the United States), it consumes the months following the death. It is still plaguing my family now, robbing us from being able to grieve purely, without the added stress and tension which often can turn to anger towards the deceased who has left you to deal with the aftermath.

I looked to grief models in search of answers, support and guidance. The grief model and theory that resonated the most for me was the Tonkin Model, developed by Dr. Lois Tonkin. I actually *really* liked this one, and as soon as my therapist had explained it to me I honestly felt relief and happiness.

In brief, it basically advocates the sentiment that my grief may stay the same, but my life will grow around it. Finally a model that isn't holding hands with the cliché of 'time will heal' or pushing me to get over it, something that still seems so impossible, but rather acknowledging that though I might not move on from grief, my life will go on and I will expand my life around it.

So what is the model? Basically draw a circle - this represents your life - then shade in the circle, which represents the grief you are feeling, how it's overwhelming and enveloping your life. As time goes on, rather than the shaded area becoming smaller, indicative of you getting over the death of a loved one, something that doesn't make sense, your outer circle expands and effectively grows around the grief. It acknowledges that grief is not a 'complete' process. The process of mourning does not end in completion.

I visualise this model a lot in my head, most of the time at night before bed as a way of checking in with myself and seeing how I was feeling and coping, like a conclusion to my day. On some days, especially in the first few months following dad's death, my outer circle was tightly aligned to the shaded mass. The grief was all-consuming.

On other, happier or busier days, I'd visualise a bigger circle around the shaded area. This was definitely not a linear process and the space between the shaded grief and the outline circle didn't get greater every day. It ping-ponged back and forth a lot between depending on whether I'd had a good or a bad day. Models of grief and how they resonate with you is intensely personal and you may find that you disagree with many things I have written in this section, but personally, I found the Tonkin Model enabled me to generally just have a happier outlook on life.

The analogy which has remained at the forefront of my mind since I first heard it, and is my go-to when I need to explain to someone how I'm feeling, is an analogy of traffic lights. It is also the title I have given to this book. In one of my bereavement sessions I explained to my therapist that I was scared for time to be moving on because though I didn't want to wallow in this time period forever, or risk people thinking I wasn't helping myself by mentally staying in this time and space, I was scared that as time went on memories of dad would fade, his voice would grow softer in my head, the feeling of him scratching my back would grow more abstract and the smell of him on clothes would wash away. I was scared to let go.

My therapist explained this feeling back to me in terms of traffic lights. I was to imagine dad and I were on a stroll, perhaps walking to the shops to pick up something good to eat or as dad would say, *'something delicious, nutritious to make me feel ambitious'*.

We'd walk along, taking in the smell of the hot LA air mixed with the scents of jasmine, jacaranda and bourgainvillea and point at the hummingbirds darting between the flower heads, and feel relief from the sun when the palm trees swayed offering us breeze.

We were walking and talking and laughing until we came to a crossroads, or a set of traffic lights. We wait patiently for the lights to turn red for the traffic so we can cross. We probably would make a remark about a little dog sitting in a pushchair on the other side of the street as is quite common in Los Angeles, and dad would probably have put his hand on my shoulder and pretended to massage it asking if I'm tense saying he needs to make it 'loosey-goosey'.

Maybe he'd even start doing what he called his 'funny walk', the act of raising his leg up at a 90-degree bent knee angle, really high, and walking around like that. Something he found irrationally funny and something I found completely embarrassing as a child and most of my teen years. It only began to get funny for me once I was old enough to walk away and pretend I wasn't with him.

The traffic would start to slow as the light passed through orange to red. We'd be given the signal that we were able to cross. I step out into the road off the kurb and begin walking to the other side, just getting my foot to the pavement as the lights turn green again for the cars. I look to my side, dad isn't there. I look behind me, he didn't make the light. He can't cross. He stands there looking at me from the other side. He tells me to go on, to keep on walking, one foot in front of the other.

We have to take grief from the obscure, the abstract and the taboo, and rehumanize it. Talk about it, examine it, even laugh about it. There is no solution, there is no textbook with answer sheets to flick to on the back pages, there is no CGP revision guide.

Experience is the best teacher and I comfort myself that when inevitably a friend loses a parent, I will be there to hold their hand and understand. The farther I walk through life, the farther I am away from the traffic lights from where I left dad in a real tangible, living breathing form. On January 25th 2019, the day I write this sentence, I am 365 days past the traffic light.

How to use this book:

As previously mentioned, bereavement is not a linear process; there is no straight line between beginning and end, if there is even an end at all. For that reason, I have structured this book by emotion and theme rather than a chronological memoir of the months between diagnosis and death and the twelve months that followed, or a month-by-month emotion report.

So, within this book, I outline the ways in which grief lived within me and manifested itself for the first 365 days following dad's passing. Grieving is extremely individualistic, you can't look to another bereaved person to see if you're 'ahead' or 'behind' in the grieving process but I hope that by reading this you may find comfort in knowing that what you may be feeling is normal. As such, some parts of this book may resonate with you, and some things not at all. This book can be read two ways, either chronologically or it may be picked up at a particular chapter if you are looking to find comfort and support from a similar emotion. I have briefly outlined the chapters here to help you do this.

Chapter one, *Our Life* is an introduction to my relationship with dad. It serves to give context to this book and insight into our life and my half and half upbringing between the Cotswolds in England and dad's Hollywood realm.

Chapter two, *'It's Shit' and Other Feelings of Grief* begins with my story. I then explore the themes of grief - crying, anger, anxiety, and cognitive challenges such as confusion, memory loss, dreams and denial. I give honest accounts of how such feelings affected me mentally and generally in everyday life. Though it was therapeutic for me to get my emotions down on paper and then in the form of this book, I wish I had known at the time that all of these feelings were normal, that I wasn't descending down a lonely spiral and that there wasn't anything wrong with me other than purely feeling the expected emotions of grief. I hope if you are going through it now, these passages offer you comfort.

Chapter three, *They Didn't Teach Me This At School* looks at why we feel so uncomfortable talking about death and how it became a taboo subject. I discuss different models of grief explained to me by grief counsellors. Lastly, I explore the physicality of grief such as stress, physical pain and chronic exhaustion.

Chapter four, *'Wisdom Sits In Places'* is my exploration of how place is, for me, intrinsically linked with who I am, my social worlds and in this context, with dad. How I have thought about and managed my places, as specific as my home to as broad as my city, which now have a different meaning.

Chapter five, *The Glow-Up to Grow-Up: An Identity Crisis* looks at how my life changed when my dad became ill, how my priorities reshuffled, how quickly I matured, how my outlook on life altered and how in sum, I felt my identity had changed to something I was struggling to recognize. It ends with how different self-care practices enabled me to find some solace within this time.

Chapter six, *The Lesser-Spotted-Accidental-Insulter and the Herd of Non-Bereaved* talks about clichés people may have said to you, how I reacted to these, and how relationships change as you negotiate your current mental state and how to be with those around you who have not experienced bereavement. For me, this was one of the main issues where I felt I needed a book like this as guidance and reassurance because the predominant age group of my friends is 25 and so the death of a parent, who for someone in this age range you are still dependent on in many ways, feels totally abstract. Only three of my close friends have unfortunately experienced the death of a parent so my pool of who I could talk to who would *really* understand was extremely limited. It was during times when I desperately needed to talk to someone that I felt the most isolated and felt the need for a book such as this the most.

Chapter seven, *A Tale of Two Cities – Culture Clashes and Livestream Funerals* is my account of dad's funeral and negotiating cultural and religious differences between family members. I also explore how digital platforms and social media impact the dying and bereavement process.

Chapter eight, *Lasts and Firsts* begins with an exploration of time in an attempt to understand the relationship between temporality and emotions. The rest of the chapter recalls my feelings of the last Christmas and New Year with dad, and then the first of those events without him, as well the anniversary of his death and visiting the memorial park.

By way of conclusion is my chapter, *My Year in Hindsight*. This is a rambling of my musings of looking back over the year, how I've changed and what I wish I had done differently. There is no conclusion in a traditional sense to this book because I am still working out what my conclusion to all of this is and whether mentally I need to have one at all.

Furthermore, as grieving is such a personal experience, my conclusion would be different to yours. In a way it abruptly ends just as my dad's life had. I also feel that conclusions are very final whereas adapting to life without a loved one is an on-going process that will continually change as your life weaves through time.

OUR LIFE

To help make this book make sense, it is necessary to understand what my life is like without my dad, how important he was to me and the story of our relationship.

Dad was 50 when my twin brother and I were born and had had quite the life before we came along, and consequently had the best stories. Having an 'older' parent was never an issue, dad could run around a basketball court better than the younger men he played with. In the pool he could swim long stretches underwater quite easily being my 'dolphin' or 'surfboard' (depending on whether the lady with the perm was in the pool or not, *'no splashing'* seemed to be the only vocab she knew).

Dad gave the best back and head scratches and succumbed very easily to *'please can you just do that for a bit longer?'* He made up copious amounts of characters, voices, accents and mannerisms including 'ze doctor' and 'Mr D' which never failed to make me laugh, even as an adult. Dad had his own way of speaking around us too, adding 'ski' to the end of many words, such as *'just a minute-ski,'*, *'food-ski'* and *'Mrs butt-in-ski'* or greeting us with variations of *'howdy-doodle', 'howdy howdy'*, and *'lotz a hotz'*.

Dad was a Hollywood television and film producer and so worked away from home most of the year. In effect, mum was a sort of single parent, and dad was a larger-than-life, almost mythical figure in La La Land, working in the film business. It was bit like how Tracy Beaker idolised her absent mother, a glamorous actress making it big in showbusiness, although my dad was anything but absent.

We spoke to him on the phone every day for as long as possible and as we got older and technology improved we'd Skype a few times a week and email back and forth as much as the time difference would allow. As a child, much of the time on the phone with dad was dedicated to writing stories. I'd relay the prose over the phone and he'd furiously take notes or record the phone call with a tape recorder. I'm not actually sure what happened to them, but I do remember a few of the storylines quite clearly, full of adventure and mystery. I used to love these types of phone calls,

14

although this was also before I had any reasonable idea of international phone rates.

As a child I revelled in hearing his stories of what was happening on set or what would be taking place in the next episode of the show he was working on, or the glee I would feel as a child hearing him tell me a signed autograph to me from the actors was in the post. As I got older, I still enjoyed hearing his stories and being able to have proper discussions with him. Hearing how he'd joined the circus was always amusing, and even better - that at age 21 he had become the stage manager for a show in Las Vegas named 'Panties Inferno'.

Dad and his pals were 'old Hollywood', working from the 60s to the present day, his gang all had the good old stories and frequently lamented about how Hollywood wasn't what it used to be. If timings worked out, when my brother and I would visit him he'd always try and get us involved in some way, whether it was helping out in the production offices, unpicking seams for wardrobe departments, imitating children's drawings for art departments or being involved as an extra - it was always fun and an escape from everyday life growing up in the Cotswolds in England.

Within dad's old Hollywood pack were other producers, directors and writers; the most glamorous of hair stylists with an old Hollywood client list which would set anyone's jaw dropping, (think Joan Collins, Roger Moore, and Grace Kelly); the coolest and best of special effects, (his warehouse was the best playground and where I had the pleasure of sugar-glass being smashed over my head which obviously turned into an elaborately embellished story full of danger and bravery as I relayed it to my friends in the school playground); the hardest and most ridiculous of stuntmen, (think gorilla chest-pounding to restart his pace-maker in a restaurant. My brother and I staring with bemused fascination, and my parents calmly sipping their wines, this was normal behaviour). One of his notorious lines after someone stated how messed up his body was, he replied, *'yeah, but I had a great time getting this way'!*

Finally, a master animal handler and trainer from whom I've learned valuable life lessons such as how far snakes can launch themselves at you, what to do if you encounter a bear, how to show a wolf pack who's boss, and much play time with young chimps and baboons. One of my favourite memories as a child is arriving at a restaurant in Los Angeles for dinner and said animal trainer arriving with a snow leopard in the backseat, quite a shock for the valet parking attendant! Although another time he also took his fully-grown tiger for a walk through the *24* offices, so he's one full of surprises!

We keep dad's awards in the downstairs loo at our family home in the Cotswolds. This isn't done in a showing off way knowing that this bathroom would be the one visitors, workmen and the electrician would use. It was because it was the room we used the least, and not wanting to be too extravagant displaying them in the living room, the awards were hidden away on the windowsill above the sink. *'Well, it is where you produce'* dad would say. Quite right. There's something quite ironic to sit on the toilet and have an award reading 'Producer of the Year' staring at you.

Dad loved to take my brother and I around his work, showing us what was happening and why, although I must admit being taught about what was happening on set was much more interesting than having budgets explained to me.

There was always quite an excitement if dad let us accompany him on night shoots. The best of these was for the scene in the pilot of *24* when the female villain jumps from the plane before it explodes. My mum, brother, cousin Hannah and I were huddled on deckchairs in the balmy Los Angeles evening air, I believe somewhere around the Ventura Hills, eagerly waiting for the big moment when the two stunt women would jump out of two planes above us. Before they took flight, dad introduced us and they took my brother and I grappling on the rocks for a little while and I remember being in awe of their action skills, bravery and cool outfits. Aged nine, this was a real 'girls can do anything' childhood moment.

I decided to fly over to Los Angeles to surprise dad for his 71st birthday. As luck would have it, he was due to be filming a big action scene that week for the television movie *The After*. In the days running up to me flying out he discussed the ins and outs of the scene over the phone - how two helicopters would crash, the panicked dialogue, and where the extras would be running. Frequently telling me if I were there, I'd have a lot of fun being part of that shoot.

I'd arranged the big surprise with the help of his then assistant. The plan was that during a production meeting she'd announce his birthday and say that she'd received a present from me to give to dad only to have 'forgotten' it, at which point I'd burst through the door and shout *'Happy Birthday'!* The plan was nearly foiled by passers-by asking if I was lost as I hovered outside the room and having to just shake my head silently so dad wouldn't pick up on an English accent, but in the end it went swimmingly. There were cheers and tears and a lot of laughter.

A few days later I was in the heart of the action-filled scene dad had been telling me about. There were about two-hundred extras that day but luckily, thanks to my connection, I had a little boost in visibility. My first scene of the day was playing the mother of a small girl walking through a large foyer holding a red balloon with a few extras around us.

The next scene was the helicopter crash where all two-hundred extras and the main cast had to run down the street in terror. Some of the extras had cottoned on to my boosted camera time having watched the scene I was in earlier in the day, and my ability to have lunch with the crew, and were sticking to me like we were doing a mass three-legged race in the hope they'd be seen on camera. Running on the other side of me, the aforementioned master animal trainer, having done some stunts himself, had been roped in to be the man who got set on fire. It all made for a dramatic, fiery scene, and one that definitely tested my fitness levels!

I think my brother and I's piece de resistance was for a scene in *24* where we had the complex and critically acclaimed role of pressing an elevator button. We had to stand and watch the elevator arrive, marvel at none other than Dennis Haysbert, aka. the President of the United States and his secret service entourage get in it, give him a quick wave, wait for the doors to close and then go and press the elevator button.

I never questioned why two child characters, (we must have been about nine) were wandering around the same building as the President, although I do remember being very sad that my preferred outfit had been vetoed and instead I wore a little blue dress with a white blossom pattern. Though pretty, it was not the option I'd imagined my big break to be in.

Most of the time dad worked in Los Angeles, but there were long periods of time, years on some occasions, where he'd be working in Vancouver, Toronto, Nashville, Atlanta and Italy. We always travelled to where he was and by doing so got to experience other cities for extended periods of time.

Vancouver was one of my favourites, a walkable city with so much to do and see both inside and outside. Here, dad was working on *Supernatural* and was in Vancouver for about four years, and so Canada became my summer holiday destination between the ages of 12 and 15. Each plane ride over I'd spend a good chunk of the flight discussing the chicken goujons with honey-mustard dipping sauce with my brother which we'd order immediately upon arrival having realised during one of our first trips out there were the best thing on the room service menu.

During his time in Vancouver the cast and crew stayed at The Sutton Place Hotel, an apartment hotel ideal for television and film crews who needed a home away from home. Looking back on it, it really was like a

19

glorified halls of residence with everyone easily accessible down the hall, and not just the *Supernatural* crew either, Pierce Brosnan was a regular in the elevator with a shaken, not stirred martini, and Rene Zellweger seemed to always be waiting for some mode of transport just outside the foyer.

I remember distinct glee that Jared Padalecki, (aka. Sam Winchester) was in the apartment next door, and between the ages of 12-15 you believe it is totally plausible that they can and will become your bff. The closest I came to this was during an episode in which a scene involved Sam and Dean Winchester looking through a photo album of the deceased woman, spoiler alert - she becomes a ghost, and needed some images of her in her youth. Enter me. A few shots of me up a tree, a few running around, and a few cuddly ones with Jared's two dogs. Obviously befriending his canine family was going to be my best chance of kickstarting our friendship. If I recall correctly, as they flick through the album the line is, 'she was beautiful'. I hope he wasn't referring to the dog.

Another excellent perk to Vancouver was that I managed to convince dad that we absolutely needed a hamster. Thus, a little hamster and the Taj Mahal of hamster cages with tubes and mazes galore became an apartment feature. This hamster being my first pet came everywhere with me, including the studio offices. Looking back, there's something quite comical about my brother and I sitting in dad's office watching films, (I distinctly remember these including *Inspector Gadget*, *Charlie's Angels,* and

Indiana Jones), whilst dad had an important meeting around his desk, and my hamster rolling around in her ball, seeds flying out of the air slits.

Every November we'd meet dad in New York City, which is where he grew up and where most of his family are outside of Los Angeles. I loved these trips as a child, full of New York winter magic, Macy's Day Parade, and a huge family Thanksgiving dinner. As a fun element, dad would send a stretch limo to pick us up, always trying to beat the stretchiness of the last one!

When I was apart from dad we were in constant contact, I didn't realise how much I relied on him in everyday life until he was gone, a constant source of comfort and company. If I couldn't sleep at night I'd send him an email as it would be his daytime, (this is how we predominantly communicated, he thought it was the same as messaging), and every time I'd wake up in the night I'd refresh my emails to see if he'd emailed me. He was basically my diary of what I was doing and vice versa - I knew what he had eaten for lunch, what he was having for dinner, where he'd just nipped out to in the car, who he was meeting with, what the weather was like, what he thought of the latest breaking news story.

I guess with living in different countries this kept us very connected. After dad died I suddenly felt very alone. If the time difference allowed, I would always call him when I was on the bus, call if I was walking home and it was dark outside, call if I was by myself and wanted some company. A lot of the time it was literally out of boredom and just wanting someone to talk to, but it was never a dull conversation.

21

I can't do that anymore. He loved our chats, even if I wasn't in a particularly great mood, and if he had to go somewhere or another call came through he'd always call back as soon as he could. I never felt like he just wanted to get off the phone. When dad died I worried that people would think I wouldn't need to grieve because I didn't see dad that much, but in reality I believe I spoke to him a million times more than if we'd all lived at home together.

He was my confidant when mum or my brother were annoying me or if I'd had a disagreement with them. If I'd bought something and felt guilty about it I'd call him and he'd always convince me that it was a good purchase, whether it was necessary or not. For want of a better phrase because I think it sounds too icky and princessy, I was a 'daddy's girl'.

At this time, memories are too painful to remember, they don't offer me comfort yet in time I know they will as long as I keep them alive in my mind. Dad and I could always make each other laugh, he found everything I did amusing and as he would say, would 'get a kick out of it'. Most of the time, though highly irritating or embarrassing, I would find his jokes or actions funny too. When dad was ill I got through it with humour, and to an extent so did my mum and brother.

We never found out dad's prognosis as a family. Mum, my brother and I knew it, we didn't know if dad knew, we never spoke about it. He got through the days by believing he would get better and that our lives will carry on as normal, we'd still go on the Yosemite trip we'd always planned as a family, and go to the next big show in Vegas, and so that is how I acted around him. I would still tell dad off if he was being annoying, or too flustered or not understanding. I didn't want him to see me upset, panicked and grief stricken. I didn't want him to think that mentally we had already put him in his grave.

In the hospital I still cracked silly jokes at him or about him and tried to make him laugh. To be honest, some things were funny in a sitcom, gallows humour kind of way. It was hard not to laugh when retelling him what he had mumbled or hallucinated, though desperately sad it was funny to hear the words he used to describe objects he could no longer remember the name of.

My favourite was 'water tweezers' for pipette. You have to laugh otherwise you'll go mad. We all laughed when about ten minutes after dad died a nurse came enthusiastically bursting into the room holding some form of apparatus declaring, 'great news, we have found something to help his lungs which will help him breathe better'… There was a moment of shocked silence before mum blurted out, 'he's dead!' and saw us laugh quite hysterically and neurotically whilst the nurse, whose face had gone from excitement, to white as a sheet, to a deep blush of beetroot edged backwards out of the door. 'Wonder how he'll retell this story?' we joked, 'bet he'll lie awake at night for a while cringing at this one'.

'IT'S SHIT' AND OTHER FEELINGS OF GRIEF

I f I had a donation jar for every time I or another person said '*it's shit*'

as a (normally first) response to how you feel when someone close to you dies, I'd be able to pay for the extortionate cost of dying in the United States.

Person: '*How do you feel?*'
Me: '*shit*'.

Me: '*My dad just died*'.
Person: '*that's really shit*'.

Person: *'there's nothing I can say other than it must be really shit'*
Me: *'yeah, it's shit'.*

Oxford Dictionary definition of shit:
Noun - *'vulgar slang'*
Verb - *'expel faeces from the body'*

In late November 2017 the universe defecated all over my family's life, offering us a stage-four diagnosis of lung cancer and lymphoma and double kidney failure with my dad as sacrifice. Pretty vulgar.

There I was, on an unremarkable day sat at my desk at my part-time job in central London, responding to client emails and wondering how soon I could make another cup of tea when my boredom-plea was answered by my phone ringing.

Waltzing out of the office into the stairwell I began to take the call from my mum. A few minutes later I had hung up the phone and was standing silently but with a new feeling of heaviness and nausea in my stomach. She'd told me that dad had been taken into hospital, just for a few checks, nothing serious, will probably be in for a couple of days, blah blah blah. The classic lines parents give you when they try not to set off the alarm bells in your head. That's how it all started.

A couple of days later I was lounging on the sofa at my boyfriend's flat nursing a food baby following a spag-bol when mum called again. This time to tell me that some tests had been done and we were just waiting for the results. Through her thinly veiled guises I deduced these 'tests' were testing for signs of cancer. The c-word. We didn't discuss it further, there seemed to be no point, because obviously that was not going to happen to anyone in my family, and by talking about it we might jinx it and bring it upon ourselves.

With building levels of stress and anxiety I went back to nursing my bloated stomach and flicked on the TV, probably *Strictly Come Dancing*, *First Dates* or something on Netflix, I can't remember.

Fast-forward another couple of days, (but all in the same week because cancer waits for no one) I was sat in the cinema in Malvern with my aunt and uncle who I was visiting for a few days.

Dad was having some more tests and the cinema seemed like a good distraction. The film, *The Death of Stalin*, was over around 9ish and walking back to the car I turned my phone back on...no missed calls and no messages. To avoid raising attention to my concern I sent a couple of Whatsapps to my mum from the backseat of the car on our way to the house. Blue ticks but no response.

Here is where it makes sense to tell you that though I was based in London, but on a visit to Malvern, my dad was in Atlanta working and my mum flown out for a visit, perhaps serendipitously eerie in timing. Around 10:30pm the landline ran. Who calls at this time of night if not a family member or someone bearing bad news? It wasn't my house but

I darted to the phone, and my aunt was the first to speak to mum and shut herself in the kitchen out of earshot, emerging a few minutes later and handing me the phone.

This time the c-word had changed to a capital. Cancer. The fluffier parts of the conversation have left my memory but the keywords have remained like thorns in my skin. *'It is cancer darling, and I'm afraid it's stage four, there's nothing we can do'*. I can't recall the next few minutes other than shuffling about and somehow sitting uncle-me-aunt on the sofa all in silence with newly filled (to the brim) glasses of red wine. Silence, numbness, no tears, no disbelief because it hadn't sunk in yet. I went to bed.

The next day passed in a blur, no one knew what to do or what to say, we carried on as if we'd never found out. The difference was that cancer stories on the radio seemed louder and more pronounced, cancer adverts on the TV seemed to last forever and be constant, and once back in London, cancer, death and funeral care adverts on tube platforms seemed to plague me wherever I looked up. I made my way back to London from Malvern on the train. I felt as if I were on drugs, nothing felt real, everything felt as though it was closing in on me, no one on the train beside me felt tangible as if my hand could pass straight through them if I reached out.

Conversations seemed louder, the travel tannoy seemed more invasive and piercing and I felt pain. I felt irrational and sudden disdain towards everyone around me who I now believed to have perfect lives as mine had begun to shatter with no hope of taping back together. I felt out of place, not comprehending how the people around me could be chatting, smiling, laughing. I got off at Euston and made for Richmond. I hated everyone on the tube. I hated everyone on the bus. I counted the steps from the bus stop to my boyfriend's flat and once inside I couldn't fathom leaving again.

Flash forward a week or so to the 28th November 2017 and I was in Atlanta, 'surprise' visiting dad in hospital so he wouldn't think I'd flown out on a death-watch. He lay in the bed at Emory Hospital in and out of a hallucinatory state, only the beginning of the appearance of dad, *my* dad, had began to ebb away. For myself, my brother and my mum the next 59 days of our lives were filled with the interiors of hospitals, meeting doctors, chasing doctors, asking doctors, medical phone calls, ambulances, hospital-to-hospital flight transfers, three-in-a-bed nights, dialysis centres, paperwork…so much paperwork. There was no time to cry, no time to take stock or understand what was happening to our lives.

Dad passed away on the 25th January 2018 in hospital in Los Angeles.

We got through it by trying to find humour in the chaos, finding similarities between doctors and fictional characters, and idly sketching appointments when waiting for delayed consultants in the notebook I was in charge of writing in.

We laughed about things dad had said like finding the monkeys he claimed were running around the ward during his visionary periods, he'd joke with masked nurses about what banks they were about to rob and whether he could come too, to a palliative care doctor Googling him and confessing his admiration.

We laughed hard at the time dad thought he could ring through his lunch order whilst we weren't in the room only for the chefs to be clued up on his strict cancer and renal dietary requirements, promptly delivering his burger which consisted of a large romaine lettuce leaf, a square of orange cheese on top with a piece of onion on top of that…no meat, no sauce, no bun. *'This diet is going to kill me,'* he'd say, shaking his head and shuffling the food around.

In truth, for the few times he was out of hospital, mum and I thought shopping in supermarkets for food that adhered to his extremely restrictive diet would kill us, yet the feeling of relief I experienced when food shopping after dad's death, and the freedom to buy whatever i wanted, left me feeling guilty for many supermarket trips to come. Other necessary tasks such as cooking, washing up, cleaning, doing the laundry, topping up my Oyster card and so on felt totally mundane and irrelevant, they seemed so pointless and small. Everything was a mental struggle.

'Rest now because as soon as you land, you'll hit the ground running'

Mid-January 2018 I flew from Los Angeles to London. The doctors had told us dad probably had another six months or so and so it was the right time for me to go home, update the family, reconnect with my boyfriend and friends, check in with my part-time job and set up a meeting with my PhD supervisor.

I was home for less than two weeks when my phone rang at 7am on Wednesday 24th January where I was lying in bed at my best friend's house in Brixton after a salsa lesson the night before and a girly weeknight sleepover. An evening of fun, *real* fun that I hadn't experienced since November, a small respite from what I had been dealing with and what was going on on the other side of the world.

It was my mum; dad was going and reading between the lines, I would not be able to get back to Los Angeles in time, *'are you sure you want to fly out?'* she said. The magic was broken, I was hurled back onto the ride. The rollercoaster that had swept me off my feet a month or so beforehand and taken me through numerous uphill climbs and loops had caught me again.

Within a few hours my friend had Ubered me off to my cousin's house in southeast London who had packed me a suitcase, brought me some plane snacks and driven me to Heathrow airport. I was soaking wet because it was torrential rain and I needed to find a toilet-stop en route

31

which saw me running through Battersea to public toilets, two locations were out of order and the third, a pub took pity on me and allowed me to use their facilities.

From Heathrow I called my boyfriend, *'I've got to go back, will call again when I'm through security'*, I called my work, *'I'm at the airport, I won't be in for a while, I'll email you'*, I emailed my PhD supervisor, and then I screeched, *'are you joking?!'* to an airport worker at the gate who refused to let me board until I had removed my glasses to check my face against my passport.

Settling into my flight a wave of excitement about being on a plane rushed through me, the type you feel when you're going on holiday, although within a split-second reality came back to me and the adrenaline that had kept me going all morning absolutely disappeared and I completely lost it as the plane hurtled down the runway. I was a sobbing, shaking mess by the time the seatbelt sign had come off and my mind flicked between utter heartbreak and embarrassment at my meltdown, partially due to not wanting fellow passengers to think I was a nervous flyer when in fact I pride myself on being a frequent flyer, long-hauls being my speciality.

I made my way to the back of the plane where I found a group of cabin crew preparing. I barely croaked out a request for a glass of orange juice for the sugar before my body crumbled, tears had taken over my face like the collapsing of a dam and a member of the crew had held onto me with the others rallying around.

I explained my situation to them and they comforted me at the back of the plane until I had somewhat calmed down. The cabin crew were Amy, Nicole, Roxie and Andy flying for Air New Zealand - their names and faces have been engraved in my mind since the flight in January. These four people were my guardian angels and I do not know how I would have made it through the twelve-hour flight, not knowing if my dad had passed away or not, without them.

I vividly remember Andy telling me that they had found an empty seat in business class for me so that I could try and rest because *'as soon as you land you'll hit the ground running'*. His words stuck with me and he was right, I hit the ground running not only to the hospital, but for the rollercoaster of events that followed.

Having moved my belongings to Business Class, they escorted me to my new seat which they had turned into a bed. The seat they had found was at the front of the section, telling me that this way no passenger could see my distress and assured me I would be first off the plane when we landed. For the remaining 10 hours or so of the flight they made sure I was never alone and had alerted other cabin crew to my situation.

They provided me with much-needed refreshments: chocolate for the sugar, chamomile tea to calm me, and monitored if I ate, stayed hydrated and got any rest. They perched on the end of the bed with me and held my hand in my darkest moments and treated me in the way as I imagine they would a younger sibling of theirs. They made me feel as though I was the only passenger on board that flight, and that getting me through the gruelling hours of anxiety and uncertainty was their main priority.

As we approached LAX they gathered my belongings and readied me for getting off the aircraft. When we landed however we had to wait for a short while on the tarmac before we could go to a gate. During this immense time of anxiety, they sat on the aisle of the plane next to me, holding my hand and calming me. As soon as the plane doors opened a member of the ground staff ensured I was first off the plane, escorted me through the airport, making sure I did not queue for anything by shouting *'she's a [insert code numbers I do not recall here]'* until I was out and on the way to the hospital.

I arrived at St. John's Health Center at 8pm and dad passed away at 8:14am the following morning. I firmly believe that the Air New Zealand flight I took was the last one out of London that would have enabled me to see dad before he passed away, or at least before he lost all consciousness and hearing. I will never forget that flight, moments from it play out in my head daily like flashbacks and I will forever vividly remember and be grateful to the cabin crew and ground staff who assisted me that day.

I spent the 12 hours between 8pm and 8:14am in dad's hospital room, my mum, brother and I alternating between chairs and perching on the bed whilst family and friends who could make it to the hospital came in to say goodbye and bring us refreshments. Through the night we experienced an earthquake, (luckily only minor), rain, (rare for Los

Angeles), a rainbow directly outside dad's window, which overlooked the hospital's rose garden, followed by a beautiful beam of sunlight which streaked across dad's face, warming his last breaths. By 8:15am it was over.

Mum called some of dad's family, I called my English family, I called my boyfriend, I called my friends Louisa, Cezaria, Britney, and messaged a couple others. A few hours later we left the hospital and ordered an Uber to take us to dad's flat. I'll never forget that drive, how it felt leaving the hospital, leaving dad behind in it…somewhere, wondering where he had been taken, craning my neck back so the hospital was in sight for as long as possible. *'Please don't ask us how our day is going,'* I said in my head to our Uber driver.

Though I remember it, and writing these words sends tingles up my cheeks and forms a lump in my throat, I can't explain how I felt. It's not that I don't want to, it's just that I still haven't found the words, perhaps we don't have words for such an experience in our language. This thought makes me ponder the parallel with an extinct language which we have never had the use of needing to converse about technology, landing a man on the moon, or the language to book a shellac or balayage appointment. Perhaps we haven't developed the ability to put into words how we really feel at such traumatic moments.

I remember thinking how am I supposed to feel? How do I spend the rest of the day? What am I supposed to do? I messaged a friend who had lost a parent asking them. *'You don't have to do anything,'* they replied. I clicked my phone off and sat quietly in the back of the car looking at the houses passing by the window, the familiar streets which suddenly seemed so foreign. We were all silent, I couldn't bear to look at my mum or brother.

I can't remember getting out of the Uber or unlocking the door to the building or hauling my suitcase up the stairs to the door of the apartment. I remember walking inside. I remember a weird nervousness and hesitation, the kind you feel when you first walk into a hotel room and hope it looks like the pictures on the website rather than being paired off with the least desirable room. Or when you walk through the door of a flat viewing you're looking to rent, an air of anticipation but fundamentally the feeling of walking into a strange, unfamiliar and cold place. I got in the shower, dug out my pyjamas from my suitcase and fell into bed. I lay there, exhausted from the flight and jetlag, exhausted emotionally, exhausted from my brain endlessly trying to work out what had just happened and what I had just witnessed, trying to work out what would be next for me, as if my inner workings were a computer trying to fix a big glitch in the system.

Shock, surrealness, disorientation and denial has been a constant feeling since leaving the hospital for the last time and I feel as though I have lived every day of the first year in this state. At times this has manifested itself as total confusion but for many more, and especially the days and first few months following dad's death, I found myself carrying on with life as if nothing had happened.

I don't think I cried, or at least properly cried, until March. It wasn't that I didn't care or was unaware of my circumstance, it was just that my brain hadn't caught up with reality, truly realising that my dad had just died wasn't in my ability yet. I still wonder whether I truly realise this now. It is easier to pretend that he's going to call soon. It wasn't that I was refusing to believe it had happened and was in denial even when everyone around me was talking about it, it was just that I still was so sure that this kind of thing does not happen to me, and therefore, quite simply, it just couldn't have happened - what a big horrible dream this has all been but I can wake up now and go down for breakfast with dad at the table.

Waterproof Mascara

Waterproof mascara - I recommend a purchase. I recommend it because though you think you may not cry in public, you will. You absolutely will. I cry in the most unlikely of situations and places. I am pretty shy, have moderate social anxiety and find most things utterly embarrassing or anxiety inducing.

My most vivid memories from having music lessons at school, (we were a three-instruments-each kind of a family), was not the beautiful music I learned to play or the scales I practised and memorised for hours on end. No, it was the total sick feeling of having to either raise my hand to ask the teacher if I could go to my music lesson, or standing outside classrooms plucking up the courage to open the door and go to my seat after my music lesson which would obviously involve walking in front of everyone in the classroom to my desk (mega cringe) and before that, potentially opening the door the wrong way or, because my school building was very old, it being really stiff and difficult to open (embarrassing).

Don't even get me started on hauling my cello through the school and onto the bus. At 25 I'm only five-feet-tall, imagine what this was like circa 12 years old - a 2006 12-year-old.

I digress, but the point I am trying to convey is that I do not like doing things that draw attention to myself, so you can imagine my horror when I found myself crying *everywhere* but in my own home. I cried at my part-time job many times. I think in part because I didn't have enough distractions but coupled with it being embarrassing to cry in front of my colleagues and the fact my desk was the farthest away from the toilets, it just made it worse.

I cried all the time on the 371 bus and the Northern Line. So much so I often wondered whether I had almost inadvertently made it a learned behaviour of sorts and now that was all I could do on them. I think I cried on public transport the most because it was doing something mundane but surrounded by the bustle of everyone around me getting on with their busy lives.

I think the last time I'd cried in public before this was sitting at the bar of Rosa Mexicana in Manhattan in November 2016 watching the results of the first few States roll in all going to Trump. My eyes bulged at the screen in disbelief, my hands caressing my Hillary badges pinned to my jacket, stinging tears escaped my eyes and the bar man slid an on-the-house pomegranate margherita down the bar towards me.

I felt a lot of hopelessness and despair but I knew I had to give myself permission to grieve and not feel as though I was being indulgent. I didn't have to rush back to my part-time job or throw myself back into my previous social world of meeting up with friends as much as I could. I was allowed to say no to social events and importantly, not feel guilty for doing so, this is definitely something I had to learn as I always hated letting people down.

I felt isolated in my grief from having to pretend I was getting on with life like normal, business as usual, get up, get dressed, get on the bus, get to work. But this wasn't the case for me anymore. We adapt to the loss of a loved one, but we continue to feel their absence, like the loss of a limb.

I couldn't listen to music for months and sometimes I still struggle with this. Anything would set me off, whether it was a sad or slower song, which I actively tried to avoid anyway, or an upbeat song. It's like when you've got music on and you're looking longingly out of a car window as the world blurs past you and rain drops streak diagonally along the pane and you're pretending to be in a sad music video, but I don't even have to pretend to be sad now.

I have silent showers because sobbing in the shower trying to sing along to songs like Wheatus's *'Teenage Dirtbag'* on a Spotify throwback playlist often left me totally exhausted. Blubbing is definitely not conducive to trying to get out Hanson's *'MMMBOP,* and don't get me started on James Arthur's *'Say You Won't Let Go'.* Sob. Fest.

You also can't escape accidentally overhearing vignettes of other people's lives and their experiences with death. When this happened to me I found it immediately triggered anxiety as well as opened the floodgates of my eyes. No matter how hard I tried to block out what I was hearing or no matter how quickly I could get away, it had hit me and had pierced the water balloon.

I remember standing on an overcrowded commuter train into London Waterloo, standing over the four seats which face each other and hearing one passenger tell his friend that his dad was imminently dying and he

40

was on his way to the hospice but was trying to decide whether or not he wanted to witness it. I couldn't move away because the train was so full, all I could do was stand and stare, I wanted to shout out that I knew what he was going through all the while having an internal debate with myself about whether given the choice again would I want to be there for the final moments or not. Another time I was in a doctor's surgery waiting room when two older women were discussing their husband's deaths in great detail, both of whom were vehemently happy their husbands had died at home. I wanted to shout at them to shut up and didn't they know that my dad had just died a month before and in a hospital surrounded by the sterile walls and invasive noises they were so glad their husbands had avoided.

Instead I buried my face in a little information booklet and let the tears stream down my cheeks under cover. In all honesty, and selfishly, I think I'm glad dad died in hospital. I can't imagine him dying at home and the panic I would have felt not knowing what to do next. I literally would have had no idea. I was grateful for the nurses that came in to the room when dad died in hospital, though their 'tests' to make sure dad was really dead seemed quite brutal at the time, I was glad of their supportive hugs and telling us what would happen next.

Another time I had stepped off a train at Waterloo station to hear a busker singing a medley of hits from *The Phantom of the Opera* and *Les Miserables*. '*Wishing you were somehow here again*' and '*On my own*', I mean seriously, what are the chances, and what made it worse was that she had a beautiful, high voice that went straight through me. If you've been to Waterloo during rush hour you know how big it is and how crowded it is that its impossible to move anywhere fast. I literally could not get away from the songs. I fought my way to the side and slumped down a wall, I'm pretty sure I stopped breathing for a little while. I felt despair, utterly hopeless and felt like I couldn't get up, my legs felt completely paralysed. I wanted to curl up in a ball right there on the floor in the middle of everyone and go to sleep. Severe hibernation instinct.

The lump in my throat, the stinging feeling in my face and behind my eyes, (like when you hit your nose or get it pierced…sorry mum) and the welling of tears occur when I'm busy and distracted or feeling fine, relaxing with friends. I can be gleefully skipping around Tesco with my best friend, picking out ingredients for our mac and cheese when grief will strike again, or if I've nipped out to the shops for some breakfast essentials and I'll feel the splatter of a hot tear on my palm as I count out correct change for the cashier.

Grief really goads me; it comes up in socially inopportune moments or when I'm enjoying my day and it can come from nowhere, manifest quickly and hit me hard, taking the breath out of me and often leaving me a crumbling mess.

I cried a lot during my grievance counselling. Between sessions I would frequently feel as though I were a pressure cooker, storing up emotions without allowing an outlet for them, (other than when I'd spontaneously cry). Having to verbalise and make a noise out of recalling what had happened seemed impossible to do without crying but it was within this space that I felt comfortable doing so and it acted as a release. I could sob through a sentence with tears running into the snot running from my nose and then meekly apologise for causing a fuss and reach for a crumpled Costa napkin in my bag and feel a bit better.

New Year, New Me: Anger, Anxiety and Anguish

After dad died I noticed changes in my personality and emotional well-being. I was angry and I was anxious. I found I had a much lower tolerance to noises and crowds, which often felt like physical pain or incessant drilling into my head, I couldn't cope with the hustle and bustle of day-to-today city life in London. It made me feel as though everything was closing in on me.

I found panic attacks and anxiety attacks would pounce at any moment, whether I was actively thinking about my grief or not. I could be in the middle of a conversation at work when the rising vomit feeling in my throat and uncontrollable body shakes would hit. I could be singing in the shower when the wind would be taken right out of me, rendering me breathless in a heap on the bathroom floor.

I could be paying for shopping when the grief hits my soul and explodes out of my eyes. I could be on the bus listening to a podcast or reading over my university work when the palpitations and sweats take over. Anxiety and panic took various forms for me, and it could strike at any moment. For a while I didn't want to leave the house or go anywhere out of my comfort zone or be near people I didn't want to see me cry, just in case. I felt like it was something that had to be endured alone.

I had been brought up in a society that insinuates it is socially unacceptable to cry in public or to attract attention to yourself, or to voice how you were feeling or that you were hearing voices or talking out loud to dad, I didn't want people to think I was 'going mad'. Yet I learnt 'you can't fight crazy', I couldn't fight the anxiety fire or try and reason and apply logic to it. What I could do is work through a set of things that made me feel calmer in those times, whether breathing exercises, mental exercises, taking a shower, making a phone call. You have to let the anxiety ride out, smothering it will only make it worse.

During and after this time I never felt scared to get close to anyone for fear of losing them, but I did think everyone in my life would suddenly get cancer and die. I wasn't exempt from this thought either. It made me more anxious to think about how strongly I feel for some people in case one day they're gone, but also come to terms with the fact that that will inevitably happen. No one is immortal. My best friend hadn't messaged in a couple of hours - dead or dying. My boyfriend wasn't home yet - dead or dying. A friend had a routine doctor's appointment for a repeat prescription of the contraceptive pill only to find they were dying, perhaps already dead, my female friends and I all hit 25 which meant our first smear/cervical cancer tests, all of us - dead or dying. I once asked a nurse if she could do any *all over body tests to check that I don't have cancer please?*, she looked at me bewildered and said that it wouldn't be necessary.

The fake arguments I'd have in my head about a hypothetical situation whilst showering were soon replaced by rehearsing what I would do if time were to repeat itself and I'd have to go through it all over again, or worse, if time carried on and it were to happen again, soon, to another family member. Anxiety rising and in the grip of turmoil in my head, I'd look down at my body to find my skin red from the water I'd let scold me and my fingers wrinkled from being wet for too long.

45

The only time I felt panic and anxiety between November 2017 and January 2018 was the day in November I spent in Malvern ,waiting to hear what dad's test results would show. All other times, even listening to doctors give their opinions, or doctors telling us that tests hadn't worked, chemo wasn't an option, immunotherapy wasn't an option, I was calm. I nodded at them, thanking them. Nothing inside me was screaming, yet. I think maybe cognitively I knew there was literally nothing I could do, or anyone else could do, to stop the inevitable that was hurtling towards us and so there was no use panicking. Perhaps panic is only a necessary vessel to propel you into motion when there is something that can be done and time is of the essence.

Since dad passed, anxiety and panic attacks have been a frequent occurrence and something I have learned to live with, even expect. Some days I wake up with such a debilitating feeling of anxiety, panic and doom I can't fathom going on with my day. These intense feelings are the ones I presume I should have felt during the time between the diagnosis and end of life, and are compounding now as my body is beginning to absorb and digest what has happened.

Seriously, 'hell hath no fury like a woman scorned' and all that, I suddenly became angry and irritable at everything; the cancer; the doctors who missed it and let it get to stage four before picking it up; the doctors who could not do any more; and the healthcare system in the US.

I was angry at people close to hand: the person who took the last seat on the tube before I got on; the person in front of me taking too long to pay for their shopping; the person who called me at work and took too long on the phone and wouldn't just spit it out; the person who didn't hold the door open for me; the people walking too slowly in front of me down Oxford Street when I desperately need to walk fast and with a purpose to keep my day a bit hectic to stave off any wandering thoughts of hospitals, cancer, dad.

No one was safe from the judgements in my mind and like Arya Stark from *Game of Thrones*, I had a list of names who I felt had wronged me the most, I admit generally unintentionally, but unfortunately for them, they had said or done something that I had found incredibly grating or inappropriate. Repeating their names in my head during my times of greatest emotional turmoil proved to be cheeringly calming. 'Joffrey…Cersei…Ilyn Pane…the Hound…' I'll refrain from listing my names.

Perhaps in the same vein as the new-found anger burning inside of me was the feeling of severe lack of empathy. I honestly just didn't care about anyone else's problems. I physically couldn't, there was nowhere for caring about others to be crammed into my head. Exhibit One: when friends would declare that they'd had 'a really bad day'. *'Haaaaaave youuuu?'* I'd think internally, refraining from sarcastically tilting my head to the side and uncurling my mouth from a bitchy-pout.

Of course I want to be supportive and be there for my friends who had given so much to me and let them vent about their bad days, but in these times I almost felt territorial over having a bad day. I felt bad for them that they'd had a bad day, but I just couldn't deal with it. Something that

47

would cause particularly flustered irritation was if I had said previously I was fine, to be met with *'ohh good...I've actually had a really bad day'*. It felt like Top Trumps, a game that I would always win, and weirdly took comfort in winning. Being the leader of the 'I've had the worst thing happen to me' game, untouchable number-one spot. The trophy was an all over one-size-fits-your-body-exactly, inside and out, reversible, shitty cloak, that by the way you can't take off, not even at night or in the shower.

I'm surprised my vision isn't permanently staring into the depths of my cranium from the amount of times I've rolled my eyes back whilst overhearing someone lamenting about a bad day. There are probably a few contact lenses back there. I was recently sat in a dentist's waiting room waiting for my mum when another man piped up, in the direction of the receptionist that his boiler had just broken. *'Ohhh dear,'* she said. *'Mmmm,'* he said, *'and my car is about to give out'* he finished. *'It never ends does it?'* the receptionist replied again. *'I need to get a new dishwasher'*...another person had joined the conversation. *'Oh god'*, I thought, *'we're going round the room!'* A woman sat close to me mumbled something else she was currently put out by.

I felt like the receptionist was the emcee, a sigh and the sound of her slurping a new sip of tea signalled it was someone else's turn, like holding the conch from *Lord of the Flies*. It was my turn, *'Oh you know, [sigh], my dad's just died, I've got a pile of medical bills still to go through with mum, we've had to get rid of our home in Los Angeles and having to move house here too [sigh], and among other things our shower broke on Christmas Eve and every time we look out*

48

the window we see the disaster of the new housing estate being built in the field behind but yeah, just how it goes really isn't it?'

I only said that internally whilst pretending to turn the page on my Kindle, ignoring the fact it was my turn to dirge a misfortune, all of which were obviously made all the worse by it having just been Christmas and so such negative occurrences had dispelled the festive cheer, but you know, what else can you really expect from January? I was grateful no one had brought up a dead pet.

I Put the Kettle in the Fridge and Other Cognitive Issues

As well as anger and anxiety I came across other cognitive challenges and changes. Nothing made sense, I felt disorientated most of the time, and on some days still do. Sometimes it was due to biology, on others I feel it was of my own doing, but whichever way round, it was every day.

I felt somehow on a different plane to those around me, not on earth, getting on with my previous, normal, logical, structured daily life, and not on a spiritual plane with dad, but somewhere in the middle, trying to tie myself down to the ground whilst making sense of death and what lies beyond. It was as if I was in a dreamland, and my ears buzzed all the time and my head hummed, and blinking couldn't bring me back to reality.

They call experiences like this dissociation – something I carried on with for a very long time and even now, past the one-year anniversary, I feel I am still practising. I fear that if I re-associate myself with my reality, the flood of emotions that will come with it will be too much and will control me. I can't let myself think about dad when I am by myself and I turn off music or films if they trigger me when I am alone.

The saying 'being on an emotional rollercoaster' has never been so accurate. Exhaustingly, the lows are low and the highs are high and there's no real middle ground. Sometimes something that would be really quite minor during pre-dad dying days would now make me so high and giddy that I'd burst out crying and then the inevitable crash would follow.

One time, Taboo from the Black Eyed Peas responded to my DM on Twitter and honestly you'd have thought from my diverse reaction that I'd won the lottery and then lost the ticket. Even writing this book has been in stages, I could only do it when I wasn't home alone, fearing that whatever emotions may come up would be too overwhelming to deal with by myself.

I couldn't look at things in the same way. Old people are dead, people in the past are dead, people in museums are dead, my dad is not supposed to be, and along with it, everything he has touched whether physically or through me, has a new meaning. To me they're no longer 'living' or 'current' objects, they're artefacts, evidence of my past life that was untouched by death. My email inbox, eagerly refreshed, hoping for a message from dad. The wand on the clock striking 4pm, the time I knew dad would definitely be awake in Los Angeles, the duvet cover he would pull up and tuck me in with, the cutlery that we'd used as a family, the new item of clothing he'd never see, was still touched by him because I knew he'd never see it.

My boyfriend even managed to get me out for a run, (something I absolutely do not do) and whilst out jogging he complimented my red sneakers. *'Thanks'* I said, *'dad gave them to me. He was working on a cheerleading show and these were part of their training outfit so he sent me a pair'*. Even an unlikely possession such as a random pair of shoes was connected to dad in some way. I wanted to get rid of every material item I owned and completely start again. Perhaps a saving grace that my student budget would not allow such an extravagant activity.

51

Whilst there still isn't a wealth of scientific study into the process of bereavement, there have been some important neurological findings, particularly pertaining to the hippocampus, the part of the brain linked to emotions, mood, memory and learning. Perhaps the term 'hippocampus' became more well known after Dr. Blasey Ford's brave and ground-breaking testimony before the Senate Judiciary Committee in September 2018 where she stated, *'indelible to the hippocampus is the laughter…'* referring to her ability to distinctly remember laughter during her trauma, but not other facts such as dates.

For me, indelible in the hippocampus is what dad physically looked like, what his death sounded like, and what death looked like. Yet I can't at all recall the faces of the nurses or doctors who came into the room to confirm his death, or what my brother was wearing, or what the first thing my mum said to us was.

Blasey Ford also referred to norepinephrine and epinephrine, neurotransmitters and hormones involved with stress. Under stress, surges of these travel between neurons which ultimately either facilitate memory loss or enhanced clarity of a memory. This is why though the whole event may be traumatic, only some elements of it are remembered clearly. For me, those clear memories are deeply etched into my mind like a deep cut that stitches cannot yet aid. It's too raw, it's too open, it's too surreal.

Other than remembering traumatic experiences, I immediately suffered from memory loss. I couldn't remember dates, my address or my phone number. I couldn't remember what I'd done the day before, what I'd had to eat or even if I'd eaten. I found this sensation particularly frightening. It was as if other than dad and hospitals my brain was completely empty, a black hole. It wasn't as if information such as my phone number had fleetingly left my mind, like when you momentarily forget something, but it's on the tip of your tongue, it was as if I'd never known in the first place. After telling my therapist she told me to think of my brain as a filing cabinet and at the moment all the draws are full, they're overflowing with grief and every moment of the last two months. Everything else had been pushed out as the new memories have been squeezed in and unfortunately the filing cabinet caretaker, me, was not in any reasonable or rational position to start processing or organising all the data.

At the same time, I realised I could no longer recall memories of dad before his diagnosis. I couldn't reach those memories, they had gone and all that was left behind were the memories I made each day in the hospital with him, memories of him deteriorating day by day. I became scared to continually block out the more traumatic and painful memories I had of dad in case my memory never came back and those were all that I had left to visualise when I wanted to visit dad in my head.

Over time these memories did gradually start to come back but not until at least 10 months or so down the line. As I write this I know they are not all there yet and the 24 years' worth of memories I had before are probably less than 50 percent restored and they're not as fleshed out and vivid as they used to be, but what I had noticed was that memories that come back first were ones that held no real significance before.

They were mostly memories of me during my childhood, maybe playing a game, having a family dinner, or a phone conversation with dad. These memories were not ones I knew I had held onto. I often wondered why my brain took me back to my childhood rather than memories of dad during my teens and early 20s, the memories I thought would be much clearer, or more impactful and meaningful. Perhaps as a child you are innocent, I had no real grasp of what being ill meant, or dying. I could be care-free.

During the day, painful memories reared their head in the form of flashbacks and visions, and at night, as bad dreams or sleep paralysis. I am a person who gets very vivid and real -feeling dreams every night and I am always able to remember them. I have always been glad of this and found it exciting to think about in the morning when I woke up and explain the ridiculous adventure stories I had been on in my sleep to others.

Everyone would tell me that I was so lucky to able to remember. Once dad died this luck rapidly became a misfortune. For the first few weeks I don't recall any dreams that were not solely about dad being ill. Then gradually other dreams crept in alongside ones of dad in hospital, but they were all nightmares. I would often wake up screaming, crying, sweating, shaking uncontrollably.

I experienced many bouts of sleep paralysis, perhaps the worst or darkest part of it all was that my brain seemed to be playing games with me, fuelling my dreams with the most heart-wrenching material. I often had dreams where we were told dad was dying only to find out he was miraculously 100 per cent cured, or dreams of going to dad's funeral only to realise at the reception it was all a big joke and dad walked into the room very much alive.

I had one dream where dad was helping me put together a scrapbook of him, compiling photographs, memories and classic dad quotes so that I wouldn't forget. In a particularly disturbing dream I was renting an AirBnB with some friends and had settled into the property when we all started to hear a noise. We got on with our evening for a little while until we realised the noise wasn't ceasing and was becoming increasingly more and more attention-consuming. It seemed to be coming from behind the walls, no one knew what it was. No one except for me, I knew what it was. It was the sound of the death rattle. I woke up from that dream feeling so betrayed by my own mind, why would my brain give me such a distressing and fucked-up thing to think about? After a lot of these dreams I wondered whether dad had tried to send me a message somehow - I'd try and read into them.

When I wasn't dreaming about dad being ill, I was dreaming about every nightmare scenario you can imagine: being chased, being abducted, people dying, arguments, being dumped, teeth falling out, hair falling out, plane crashes...it was exhausting to be asleep. Haunting images in the form of dreams and visions became less frequent once I started talking about them.

I chose my boyfriend and my best friend to confide in, the two I was closest to emotionally, and in proximity to, as well as my counsellor who could offer me a neurological assessment of what I was going through.

55

She explained that this was a somewhat normal neurological response to what I was experiencing; my brain was trying to move trauma from short-term to long-term memory but getting stuck in between and therefore manifesting as bad dreams and flashbacks.

Once a good listener and good at concentrating, I now found this a challenge. A 140-character tweet would even be hard pressed to hold my attention. However I found this did not apply to everything, only to things I now deemed unimportant in the grand scheme of life. Not even my life in particular, but just in general. For example, difficulty relaxing and watching films or TV, I couldn't stop my mind from wandering and fixating on different elements of the hospital. Remembering what floor dad's ward was on, what the corridor smelled like, what the huge Christmas tree in the hospital foyer looked like, how seeing dad attached to the dialysis machine made me feel queasy.

I'd aimlessly scroll through social media apps with no purpose for longer than I'd like to admit. I often thought about digging out my old Sims games to play, at least that way, and from what I can remember from playing it when I was younger, it was pretty all-consuming and made time go by fast. The amount of times I'd only created a family and was halfway through building another dream home for my Sims before mum would call me for dinner or tell me that my screen time was over the for the day.

Some of the hardest times were the hours I spent at my part-time job. It was an office job and only two days a week and every one of my colleagues were extremely supportive and caring, but being in the office felt like physical pain. I just couldn't concentrate and I just couldn't see the point. What was point in going to work if you're just going to die anyway? What was the point in working hard if you just felt so rubbish through it and at the end of it? What was the point in putting myself through the commute everyday? It seemed so inconsequential to be replying to client emails about their issues, which also seemed incredibly mundane. It took a lot of strength and resilience to not reply to a passive aggressive email that I actually didn't care that they couldn't find their online dashboard, which is obviously not my fault and by the way, I have bigger fish to fry, my dad has just died.

It was hard to conceal the croak and crack in my voice when I'd actually have to speak to a client on the phone. I couldn't understand why they cared so much that it took me two days to get back to them rather than an immediate response, didn't they know I was busy, I had other things going on?

The only thing I didn't struggle to concentrate on and actively threw myself into doing was my PhD work. Though without a doubt the hardest and most time, energy and brain-consuming thing I had to do, it was only thing that let me escape my reality. I *wanted* to do it. Dad was so incredibly proud that I was doing it, I couldn't let him down, I had to carry on for him and for myself and for my family who were supporting me.

THEY DIDN'T TEACH ME THIS AT SCHOOL

Death as Taboo

Death of a loved one, no matter how prepared you are, is an extraordinary surprise when it happens. Yet it is part of the terms and conditions of life - you know death is inevitable but you don't really understand. You can't opt out, you can't get off the ride, and as a loved one left behind it's as if you know the tsunami is coming but you cannot leave the shoreline. Once it hits, it's swept you up and will forever affect your life.

Grieving is a dual process, on the one hand it is social – conducting medical, cultural, religious and societal actions and norms, where the deceased is removed from living society. On the other, it is psychological – funerary acts and bereavement rituals, such as sitting Shiva, work to mentally relocate the dead person, and mentally assign them as no longer living, perhaps mentally uniting them with other deceased relatives or friends.

But as death is so universal, why do people feel so uncomfortable talking about it? Why do people have no words to comfort someone who is bereaved? Surely mourning should act as a vehicle of relatedness – sharing your grief and memories with others helps to build a social context for the deceased person, and allows who you are talking with to participate in your intimate feelings of bereavement. Why is it that the bereaved person feels so many emotions they cannot explain? We're not taught how to deal with death or what really happens. What *really* happens when someone is diagnosed with cancer, when someone is about to die, what happens in the moments after they've passed, and what happens to those left behind?

A few hours before my dad passed away, already unconscious and still, I had asked one of the night nurses *'what will happen when he dies?'* and she thrust me an information booklet to read. This was the first time death had ever been properly explained to me: in the form of a folded-over pamphlet, printed lettering in the form of bullet points under some headings I can't remember.

Death doesn't just happen; it is an active process. Your body has to literally shut down. Think of it like when you shut down a laptop, it doesn't just turn off immediately, it closes or force quits all programmes that are still whirring around in the background. We aren't taught about this and we don't see this in the media. It's not like a hospital scene you see on the TV where all is calm until suddenly the vital signs monitor flat-lines and that's the end. It is much more active than that.

As I read the booklet, the nurse explained that dad's breathing would start to slow and there would be long pauses between breaths. She explained the 'death rattle'. If you're not aware of the fact a dying person has a death rattle then it is extremely distressing and disturbing when you first hear it, and realise you will continue to hear it until that person dies, as well as after death as it haunts your dreams. Literally, for me. The death rattle occurs when the person can no longer swallow and so a rattling sound is made as air moves through the airways past the build-up of saliva at the back of the throat. I was told this did not cause any discomfort to the patient. She told me to look out for mottled skin, particularly on the feet, which show slowing circulation and that death is nearing. She told me that hearing is the last sense to disappear, so talking to dad was important and it would be comforting for him to hear our voices in the room around him.

In the run-up to dad's final hours we experienced watching him pass through other end-of-life behaviours and signs. One of which was 'near death awareness', the instinctual knowledge that death is near. For dad, this manifested itself in the form of visions and seeing people like his parents, other deceased relatives and friends who have gone before. Not being aware of this, though, meant those present such as myself and other family members found this at times eerie and disturbing, sometimes funny (the feeling when you laugh with nervous undertones), and ultimately we assumed he was confused, going mad and hallucinating.

Research has shown that this is likely not the case; their visions are real and those who care for others at the end of their life should be aware of this phenomenon. We shouldn't 'baby talk' them out of it or try to snap them back to reality, but instead coax more information out of them, see if you can have a conversation with them about what they are seeing.

The Lion King, Tarzan, Cinderella, Snow White, Frozen, Hunchback of Notre Dame, Bambi and many more Disney and children's films all feature characters who have lost one or both of their parents. For the amount of death in children's movies it is shocking that we grow up aspiring to be princesses and possessing a good idea of how to achieve that, but the thought of death, how it happens, and even how to talk about it is so far removed from reality.

You hear people talk about 'aiming for a good death', but what do they mean? What is a 'good death'? In my experience death is nothing at all like what you see on TV. There is suffering, it's not the peaceful death people like to imagine. The reality is pretty grim emotionally, visually and sensorially – the sound of death, the smell of death, the sight of death and touch of death - dad's hands cold and stiffening making it harder to keep holding mine within his.

'Passed on', 'passed away', 'at rest', 'at peace', 'gone to sleep' - people tend to use euphemisms when talking about death. They are deemed less direct, less evasive and potentially less offensive. Though I use them in this book, in my reality I never did. For me, 'is dying', 'has died' and 'is dead' were the words I chose to use. They are final and they sting but they are only way I can verbalise what has happened. Dad has died, and there's nothing that can be done and so why sugar-coat it? I acknowledge how awful the situation is by using the words with the most impact. I think this is all part of talking about death being seen as taboo - instead we use flowery language and cautiousness so as to not upset the person, or protect them from a panic attack whilst thinking about their own loved ones' immortality.

I now no longer fear death. That's not to say that I don't want to live and am no longer scared to be home alone overnight, but the loneliness of death I previously thought of has gone. When I die, dad will be there and we can pick up where we left off. I wasn't scared to see a dead body, but at the time I wondered whether I should be, due to how we are conditioned to think that being around a dead body is scary.

I started seeing a grievance counsellor about three months after dad died and I believe it was one of the best decisions I could have made. I saw my session as an outlet and between sessions I would write notes on my phone of thoughts or emotions that I wanted to discuss. I wish I had kept the notes I had made after each counselling session but instead I deleted them off my phone, or threw the paper away. A few times I had dreams of my mum finding them, not that it would have been so much of a bad thing, but it felt intensely private…only to be shared with a counsellor I didn't know - they didn't know anyone I mentioned, and I would never have to see again if I wished.

Seeing a counsellor was the only other 'education' about death I received. I recommend it but recognise everyone copes with bereavement differently. I also recommend making sure you have the right counsellor for you and your needs. The first one I saw was not the right fit for me. Questions seemed to focus on trying to paint a picture of my life as a whole and I found questions such as 'tell me about your friends in primary school' totally unrelated to what I wanted to talk about and led me to dread the sessions, seeing them almost as a chore. After four sessions I changed to a different organisation. The therapist I saw next was specifically trained in grief counselling and as a result I found sessions with her much more fulfilling and I looked forward to seeing her.

Models of Grief

Cleaned up and swept under the rug. That's what we do when something is messy, or broken, or embarrassing, or wrong. We're always taught to fix something that is broken or isn't right, but this can't be fixed. We're not taught how to deal with that. Up until now I've always been able to 'sort out' or 'get over' a situation that's gone awry. The most serious emotional times in my life before this happened was a relationship breakup, either one of my own or one of my friends', it was shit, it hurt, but time did heal and you always got over it. There was always light at the end of the tunnel, and there was always the silver lining that you'll meet someone new, who is obviously way more suited to you, way more intelligent, way better looking, yada yada yada. I have yet to find a single silver lining to my dad dying. I'm too old to ever get or need another father figure.

Rather than trying to talk someone out of their grief, trying to get them to get over it, and 'fix' themselves, grieving people need those around them to help them walk through the grief, experience all of it, acknowledge it and live with it whilst surrounded by the comfort of those around them. No one is taught this in school, so no one knows how to handle personal grief or support a grieving friend. Sometimes I feel it is easier to remain quiet and pretend I am alright than to continually explain and justify my grief to those who can't fully understand or feel like I'm just after attention. I know this is mostly in my head, those who have been my unwavering support network have never made me feel like this, but I feel it nonetheless, no one wants to be cumbersome or a burden to others.

I started to give my grief a character, sometimes like a mini-me or an invisible friend. I imagined myself as Diana Ross singing *'Good Morning Heartache'* to my grief. The song personifies heartache, describes emotional turmoil and efforts to get rid of heartache, before finally accepting it'll be hanging around for a while so may as well come in and sit down.

I found the lyrics comforting because they allowed me to mentally accept that the feeling of grief and heartache would be with me for a long time and wouldn't disappear overnight. I might as well get used to it and acknowledging that for me was a big step forward in my mental healing process, acknowledging this wouldn't be a quick fix.

Sometimes I bizarrely even thought of my grief as a pet, it was easiest way for me to realise that it was something that needed to be cared for, nurtured, not ignored, and importantly, separable from me. I couldn't let it define me, I couldn't let it seep under my skin and throughout my body forever, I would have to let it go once I had reached a time where it no longer needed to be an embodied experience which I dragged with me everyday like an oversized cloak. I'm not there yet, the cloak is still on, but I take comfort in knowing that one day it will be off. That's not to say I'll be 'over it', but I'll have learnt over the months and years how to manage it, and to fully adapt it into my life.

One night, after a full day of drinks at a pub with friends followed by pizza and films, I lay chatting to a friend who had recently experienced death in his family. We could have a frank conversation with each other now our other friends had gone to bed. We talked about how we carry the grief with us wherever we go. In our exhausted, slightly drunk states our grief pets were conjured, the 'Goneranian' and the 'Lossauge dog', our take on the Pomeranian and Sausage dog. We swore at our own macabre and laughed with tears running down our cheeks. How ridiculous, we thought.

I learnt about different models of grief during my counselling sessions. I found it particularly useful to understand the neurology of grief and to have grief models as the foundation of which to build my own way of coping with bereavement, but I didn't find that they totally resonated with me. I think the main thing is to think about is how you deal with grief and how your mind processes things first, and then see how a model of grief fits into that, rather than the other way around.

In the introduction I discussed the Tonkin Model, the model of grief which resonated the most with me. Below I have outlined several other models you may find more helpful.

The first model I learnt about was the Five Pillars of Grief, also referred to as the Five Stages of Coping, DABDA, identified by psychiatrist Elisabeth Kubler-Ross in 1969. The five stages of grief are:

- Denial
- Anger
- Bargaining

67

☐   Depression

☐   Acceptance

Kubler-Ross's model was originally laid out as a linear process although she later acknowledged that everyone grieves differently and likely not all in that order. I personally didn't like this theory because the original linear intent of it was too rigid for me and made me feel like I needed to be 'on track' with my grief, and confused if I was experiencing one of pillars in the wrong order like depression before anger, and a failure if I repeatedly felt denial even after moving through bargaining. I felt this model put too much pressure on me.

I felt denial throughout the process, from hearing dad's diagnosis to writing these words. At first I didn't want to believe it was cancer, or at least as bad as stage four, there must have been a mistake, or there must be other tests that can be done. I didn't want to believe that chemo wouldn't work and that dad wasn't a match for immunotherapy. Then, long into the months following dad's death, I found I was still in denial, it couldn't possibly have happened to me. He hasn't called because he's just held up in a meeting; he's absent at Christmas because he's on scout with work; my birthday card is just lost in the post. But these feelings didn't fit neatly into the denial pillar, they spilled out into anger and depression, another reason why this model didn't really work for me, and to be honest I never really understood the bargaining stage.

The main reason why I didn't resonate with this theory is the final stage, acceptance. I hate that word. Why should I need to, or want to, *accept* that my dad is dead? I felt this was way too final and in a way, sweeping dad under the rug rather than keeping him, as much as I can, an active part of my life. I felt having to accept someone had died is also pressurising and implied that you will be 'fixed', almost like taking antibiotics which after the two-week course of tablets will render you perfectly well again and able to get on with your life like nothing had happened.

I have chosen two other 'a' words to help me; *acknowledgment* and *adaption*. For the most part when I'm not using denial as a coping mechanism, I acknowledge that dad is gone, I acknowledge everything I witnessed, and I acknowledge my feelings of grief. Acknowledging them does not mean I have to accept them. Rather than accepting dad is no longer a visible, 3D element of my life anymore, I adapt my mind-set to this new life ahead of me.

For example, and using some cliché scenarios here, rather than visualising dad walking me down the aisle when I get married, I have adapted my wedding daydreams to him not being there in person and how I may just walk myself down the aisle. Last year when I thought about what my future holds in the next ten years or so, I saw my dad playing with his grandchildren. I have adapted this scene to me telling my children about him, laughing with them about all the silly things he would do and the amazing things he did in his life. Mentally, adapting versus accepting is much kinder and makes me feel like dad is still part of my life.

J.W. Worden built upon Kubler-Ross's theory and came up with the 'Four Tasks of Mourning'. Stages being replaced with tasks which makes grieving a more active process. The four tasks are:

- Accept the reality of the loss
- Work through to the pain of grief
- Adjust to an environment in which the deceased is missing
- Find an enduring connection with the deceased while embarking on a new life

Worden did not intend for these tasks to be linear or suggest that you only revisit them once, and though I liked how the tasks seemed more of an activity I found them too rigid and absolute and took issue with task one, accepting the reality of dad dying.

In 1999, Margaret Stroebe and Henk Schut developed their model of bereavement, the 'Dual Process Model' which identifies two processes associated with grieving. These are:

Loss-orientated activities and stressors (directly related to the death), for example:

- Sadness, denial, anger
- Crying
- Yearning/reminiscing
- Dwelling on the circumstances of death
- Avoiding restoration activities

Restoration-orientated activities and stressors, (secondary losses such as changes to daily routine, relationships etc.) for example:

- ☐ Adapting to a new role
- ☐ Managing changes in routine
- ☐ Doing new things or meeting new people
- ☐ Throwing yourself into distractions
- ☐ Developing a new way of life

By this model we focus on the feelings associated with being bereaved whilst also doing restoration-orientated activities to help distract us from our loss. To use their term, we 'oscillate' between confronting the loss and avoiding the loss, both of which help us cope. I quite like this theory as it isn't linear, it doesn't really imply a timeframe and I recognised myself doing both things. I'd cry and so distract myself by cleaning the kitchen, I'd feel angry and stuck in the mental loop of replaying scenes from the hospital, so I'd distract myself by throwing myself into my PhD work. I'd feel totally crushed and exhausted from emotions so I'd distract myself by binge-watching a new TV series or lying on the sofa chatting to friends.

There are other models too such as Dr. Therese Rando's 'Six R Processes of Mourning' theory. During the process of mourning, Rando contends there are three phases, avoidance confrontation, and accommodation and during each phase the mourner comes across different R processes. These are:

- ☐ Recognizing the loss – avoidance phase – acknowledging the death.

- Reacting to the separation – confrontation phase – experiencing the emotions that come with the death.
- Recollecting and re-experiencing – confrontation phase – reminiscing and reviewing memories.
- Relinquishing – confrontation phase – recognizing that the deceased person is not coming back and your world has changed.
- Readjusting – accommodation phase – adapting to your life now, your new normal. In this stage the loss can feel very acute as you start to go back to get on with your day-to-day life.
- Reinvesting – accommodation phase – channelling emotional energy into continuing with your life and experiencing new things, achieving new goals, cultivating new friendships, etc.

Again, I had trouble accepting the linearity and finality of this model, but I did like having it kind of on the backburner, something to think about. I saw it as a useful guide of goals in a sense, rather than something I had to achieve - instead something I could look forward to or be proud of myself for doing. For example, I went back to ballet lessons, I met new people, I set myself new goals and I felt proud of myself for doing it.

One thing I realised whilst learning about models of grief is that I really liked analogies. I was really able to connect with these. I even came up with one myself, although it is slightly morbid and I think potentially influenced by the scene in Disney's *Hercules* where the Fates are cutting the Threads of Life when it is a mortal's 'designated' time to die. In my head I visualise rows of huge wooden sand-timers standing next to each other. Each one represents the life of someone close to me like family members, boyfriend, friends. Rather than the upturned sand-timers releasing a steady drip of sand into the segment below, they fill in a different way.

My analogy came to me in a time of intense anger and resentment, I resented 'in-tact' families, or criminals and others I believed were bad people and so therefore should have died instead of my dad. I realised that my thoughts that others should have died instead were driven by feelings of longing for dad and replaying good memories of him and thinking about who he was as a person, his character traits and what he offered and what he meant to me and to many who knew him, thoughts that I hope in time will turn into sources of comfort. My analogy thus began to take shape.

Though I will always feel robbed of the time I will no longer have with dad and things we will never experience together, I thought about the immense joy and excitement he churned inside me. I thought about how all of this compared to others in my life and where they would be on a scale if it were a points system. Realising that dad was way ahead of others I began to imagine what if he was gone because his sand-timer had filled up so fast, he'd given me so much. It was the only way I could begin to rationalise the unfairness of something so great being taken away so fast, and tragically, and for it to happen to dad, someone so undeserving of his fate. It's not a fully padded-out analogy and as time has gone on since thinking about this I think my attitude towards it has changed a bit, but when I first concocted this train of thought I really needed it. I was looking for any kind of analogy I could resonate with and hold onto.

'Have you felt stressed recently?' – The Physicality of Grief

I thought a survival-instinct type trait would kick in and tell me exactly what to do and how to cope, but nothing came. I picture my life from the moment we received dad's diagnosis like a road detour: the path I needed was closed; the one where my life continued as normal and dad's test results came back fine. I had no choice but to follow the detour, the road paved with deterioration, death and devastation, knowing at some point I would reconnect with the route I originally required, back to my day-to-day life. I wondered, will my life ever get back on track? Will I forever be living a parallel life to the one I would be on if my dad had lived for a few more decades?

I expected the emotional side of grief, the crying, the depression, not sleeping well but no one forewarned me about the physical aspects of grief. The excruciating and random pain streaking through my body, the heart palpitations, sore and strained throat, dizziness, headaches, nausea (so much nausea), the fact smells and tastes I once enjoyed made me gag, the feeling of being pummelled relentlessly in my chest and stomach. Generalised existential angst, memory loss and the panic attacks, and the anxiety attacks and IBS brought on by emotional stress. The feeling of windedness, no air left inside, not even enough to scream out. I had many dreams where I'd be shouting out for help but no noise came out of my mouth and my throat tightened with each push I made for noise.

For so long I felt like I'd been lobotomised, floating through life smiling emotionlessly at people, answering their questions robotically, remembering to be polite and behaving acceptably for society. It was hard to believe that I didn't look this way externally either, although my friends assured me that I didn't, other than a slightly glazed-over look in my eyes.

I made numerous doctors' appointments during the first 12 months, seeking answers and antidotes to the ailments I have listed above. I was always met with the question, '*are you stressed?*' or '*have you been stressed recently?*'. I almost willed something to be really wrong me so that I could be medicated and not told, '*ohhh, well then, it's no surprise with what you're going through that you're stressed and all these symptoms are how stress is manifesting in your body'*. I was glad to be medically 'alright', but I desperately wanted something to take away the pain.

I had to change my outlook to see bereavement as a physical wound, something that would obviously take time to heal and recover from. Reports suggest that the pain is caused by the overwhelming amount of stress hormones carousing around your body like a bat out of hell and basically stun every muscle they make contact with. But can you recover? Can you heal? Is the healing not like a piece of skin forming over and creating a scar, always a memory, always with you. Can people see it? In June 2017 I tore the hamstring in my right leg, my sciatic nerve and slipped three discs in my back whilst falling into the splits pretty hard in heels. This injury took over a year to mend with countless trips to doctors, specialists, MRIs and physiotherapy sessions. It was very painful and very boring having to wait out the injury but I did it and accepted that the recovery process would be long, so why can't I see bereavement in this way too?

Stress totally undermines your ability to cope so it really is the worst thing for bereavement but unfortunately it is pretty hard to escape it, pre- and post-death. I experienced anticipatory grief before I knew that was a term - the grief, anxiety and stress you feel before your loved one dies, which is often compounded by the fact you're actually really busy. For example, I not only dealt with trying to come to terms with dad's diagnosis and him dying and hours and hours spent in hospitals, but also everyday tasks like washing-up and needing to get to the shops to buy more laundry detergent, or stressors like financial issues, not finding a parking spot and trying to keep on track with my PhD and not fall behind.

I was diagnosed with fibromyalgia when I was a young child and have managed it throughout my life by recognising what exacerbates it and what makes it better. It is a chronic condition that includes widespread pain, extensive fatigue, concentration problems affectionately termed 'fibro-fog', stiffness, IBS, headaches and so on. The severity and amount of symptoms differ from patient to patient. For example, I wouldn't say I am excessively fatigued, but I do get tired much quicker than my friends around me, (a totally lame finding during undergrad), and there are some days where I wake up and it feels as though I've pulled a 48-hour stint of being awake.

On bad days, or flare-ups, the tiredness completely wipes me of any energy and it physically hurts to even move to the kitchen to make a cup of tea. When I was younger there were times mum would have to pull me out of bed because I didn't have the strength to lift up my body. The pain is localised around my ribs, it really hurts if someone touches my ribs, and then every joint is generally achey and sore. Again, on bad days everything hurts, everything is inflamed and I feel like every movement is as though I am a scrunched-up piece of paper that is being unfolded. If I get a cold or the flu the fibro makes it 100 times worse and it takes me a lot longer to recover.

The 'fibro' part refers to fibrous tissues such as ligaments and tendons, 'my' refers to muscles, and the 'algia' part indicates pain. Fibromyalgia, only recently becoming an 'on-trend' thing due to celebrities such as Lady Gaga speaking out about it, is medically under-researched and in avoidance of popping paracetamol everyday it's really kind of up to you to manage your symptoms and life. As grief can cause muscle and joint pain, stiffness, tiredness and so on, the boundaries then between my fibro symptoms and grief symptoms became blurred and it was hard to tell which was fuelling the other and whether they were just aggravating each other.

Many lyricists have mused whether you can die from a broken heart, and well yes, it appears you can. Takotsubo cardiomyopathy, or for us hoi polloi 'broken heart syndrome', is the effect of grief symptoms and stress on the heart function. Your heart muscle becomes temporarily weakened and part of your heart *literally* changes shape! The left ventricle gets larger and changes shape, resulting in this part of the heart being unable to pump blood around the body as well as it should. The main symptoms are chest pain, shortness of breath and potentially collapsing (pretty alarming and time to call 999 I would presume). Other symptoms are palpitations, nausea and vomiting. There isn't really a specific treatment other than being monitored, but it is temporary and eventually your heart will go back to its usual shape, but again the recovery process and time and any relapses are totally patient-dependent.

Something I found incredibly stress-inducing was planning to do anything, and then the thought of actually having to do it. This is a total 180-personality switch for me as usually I am a yes-person, I *love* a good plan, and could write to-do lists and organisation notes until the cows come home. I think the fact this was so different to how I normally am further increased my stress levels. If I wanted to meet up with someone I couldn't think straight about where I wanted to meet (other then preferably at home), but everyone has busy lives and London is so huge this was not possible.

As soon as a location was suggested I'd then immediately jump on CityMapper or Google Maps to ascertain how easy and quick my commute would be, with anything over 45 minutes or involving multiple bus or tube changes immediately caused a churn in my stomach. This included my commute into work and there were many days where I'd lie in bed not having the physical strength to haul myself up and go in. Again, it wasn't that I was being lazy or could have done with another few hours of sleep, my mental state had caused me to feel physically paralysed by the thought of having to leave and go out into the world and potentially break down in public.

I think the fact that I spent my days enveloped in feelings of tiredness, disorientation, extreme lethargy and lack of mental and physical energy made the very thought of planning or going through with a plan unfathomable. Despite this, though, I made myself do it. I knew that if I didn't, the problem would only get worse and I might risk becoming agoraphobic down the line. So instead of packing my week nights and week days with activities, I'd settle for maybe two or three things. At first even these made me feel uneasy and added to my immense feeling of unsettledness.

I'd make a task-list for the day, which included household or personal tasks as well as any outside plans. This way I could organise or compartmentalise the thoughts in my head slightly better and still be a semi-functioning human being. I found it helped if I wrote everything down, because even the small things were mentally taxing, but by writing them down I'd be able to experience happiness by ticking them off the list and at night as I lay in bed recollecting my day, I would genuinely be very proud of myself for doing so. Bonus points if an outside activity was crossed off, or a task I had been putting off for a while had gone. If I had any outstanding tasks by the end of the day I wrote them down on a fresh piece of paper to tackle tomorrow. An example list could have been:

1) Wash my hair

2) Buy milk

3) Cook a nice dinner from scratch

4) 50 sit-ups

5) Put a wash on

6) Email so-and-so back

7) Read chapters 6 + 7

8) Write notes on…

9) Go to ballet lesson

During this time I actually learnt two positive outcomes that I still practise today. The first is that I realised I sleep so much better if I just do a pressing task that I don't particularly want to do as soon as I learn about it, especially if it is time sensitive. Otherwise I'd find myself mulling it over in bed and dwelling on the fact I hadn't done it and another day had gone by. This was obviously not excellent for trying to get a restful sleep, or asleep at all.

The more I got into my daily to-do lists the more I added to them. By August, so about seven months down the line, my lists would sometimes be a whole page long, either because I was assigning myself more tasks, or I was breaking down tasks into sub-tasks. By this point as well I was in the fieldwork phase of my PhD which was entirely self-study and research so I had full control over my days and had to be very disciplined with time-management. As I wasn't sleeping well and regularly waking by 6am, rather than lying in bed feeling sorry for myself which inevitably led to a mixed-mood kind of a day, I got up earlier and got my day started.

More times than not in the week I would have completed the most pressing or arduous tasks by 11am which not only felt great and that I'd accomplished something, but also meant I could spend the rest of the day doing longer tasks such as reading an entire book for my studies and not worrying that I hadn't got much else done. This not only helped me sleep better at night but it helped me feel more alert and less anxious.

'WISDOM SITS IN PLACES'

Our sense of place comes from our individualistic experiences and is

influenced by our culture. 'Wisdom Sits in Places' is a book by anthropologist Keith H. Basso, published in 1996, which documents the significance of places in Apache culture predominantly through the lens of four individuals. The sentiment expressed in Basso's book echoed with me. I found myself not only experiencing the loss of my dad and a renegotiation of my identity, but also the strong feeling of loss of place and belonging, like a stranger in my own home and that the city I loved was no longer mine. This loss of place hit me hard and fast and I believe in years to come if someone asks me what were some of the strongest feelings during this time, I will say the sense of floating, not fitting in to a city that was once home, taken away within two months. I realise that my own history and social relationships are inextricably intertwined with place.

I was born in Los Angeles to an English mother and an American father. I lived there until I was five and then was brought back to the UK to start school. During my school years we were fortunate enough to visit Los Angeles regularly, every school holiday and many times during the school year until I began my GCSEs. I deemed my upbringing 'half-and-half'.

Dad mostly worked in LA so the city became synonymous with him and London airports became buildings filled with excitement whilst LAX departures was a place of sadness yet hope that the next few months would pass quickly so I could be out there again.

I always loved stepping out of the airport in Los Angeles and feeling the heat and smell of jet fuel smack me across the face as I gazed up at the palm trees. It was home. Main memories of returning there a few weeks later to fly back to England were of mum, my brother and I ascending the escalator to security checkpoints while dad stood at the bottom waving until we were completely out of sight. The solemnness of the twelve-hour flight and car journey to the Cotswolds where I grew up gradually dispersed as we began to breathe in the fresh countryside air and feel the smattering of rain on us as we unloaded suitcases from the car to the house. It was also home. Grandma was usually round waiting for us with fresh cups of tea and dinner prepared. I'd always persuade her to stay overnight too.

Originally I wrote 'where dad fell ill' but something didn't feel right, it wasn't a syntax error, but a fault in the meaning. To me the word 'fell' insinuated a verb that is your own fault, maybe you're clumsy, maybe you weren't looking where you were going and tripped, maybe you were looking at your phone when you fell. Dad didn't fall ill, none of this was his fault. When dad *became* ill, or at least when the cancer was picked up, he was working in Atlanta, Georgia.

My two weeks there consisted of Uber journeys back and forth between the hospital and our hotel, and waking early and calling the ward for an update of how dad was through the night before dressing and heading in. I always made an effort to look nice: makeup, different pieces of jewellery, wintery skirts and woollen dresses. I wanted to make an effort for dad so that he wouldn't see us sitting miserably next to him in miserable clothes everyday, and truthfully this one part of my day helped me to feel 'normal'. Plus the more makeup I put on, the less likely I was to cry, in the words of Kim Kardashian, '*I'll cry at the end of the day, not with fresh makeup*'. Honestly that quote got me through a lot of emotional times.

As most other patients' families were at work in the day, mum, my brother and I were often the only non-patients on the ward. Being so far away from our normal day-to-day lives meant we had nothing else to do but to sit with dad. It didn't feel like the right time to explore the city and the surreality of having to deal with our world turning upside down from a

85

hospital room by day and a hotel room by night was debilitating. I can't deny that the days were boring as well, as much as a guilty pang hits me each time I acknowledge that because surely I should not have found the days spent with dad boring, but it's true. Despite many reasons to defer or pause my studies, I found it was the only thing keeping me going and giving me something to focus on. I'd sit for hours in dad's hospital room with my mum consulting doctors and paperwork, dad watching CNN or sleeping and me researching and writing for my first year exam document.

By the 10th December dad had been given the all clear to be flown and transferred to the hospital of his choice in Los Angeles. It felt like finally we were going home, though not to England where my boyfriend and friends were, but to LA, the city that was still half of my identity. I was excited to feel the heat on my face after the snow of Atlanta and see the palm trees. Between the 10th December and 25th January dad ping-ponged in and out of the hospital, though he was mainly inside and home visits lasted no longer than 48 hours. It was in this time that *my* LA started slipping away. The city I had experienced so much joy and adventure and magic in, with and because of my dad, was leaving me as fast as he was.

I am someone that forms mental and emotional attachments to things easily and so it is no wonder that place attachment is a big deal for me, especially in the sense of that attachment being severed. As I write this sentence I picture two pieces of Velcro being torn apart, their friction palpable whilst trying to remain united. For me, the meaning of place attachment includes a physical site that has been given meaning as a result of interaction, for example, my present action at the place, my past action which I remember through memory and nostalgia, sometimes even smelling it, and ideas about potential future interactions I may have with the place.

So what happens when you return to a place that is no longer yours? Maybe this is the feeling you would get if you returned to your family home after it had been sold to a new family and they've redecorated. It's still familiar but definitely not the same, and due to that, the meaning of it has changed. Following dad's death my emotional attachments to my home in Los Angeles and Los Angeles as a city were completely changed, as well as to a lesser extent how I experienced London and my family home in England where I had predominantly grown up.

Within the first 12 months I flew in and out of Los Angeles many times, some from trips visiting family and friends, others having been away at conferences, but no matter the reason I couldn't escape the crushing disappointment I felt when the words 'welcome aboard this flight to Los Angeles' or 'welcome to Los Angeles' failed to ruse any excitement no matter how hard I tried. Perhaps the same feeling you get on Christmas Eve when you long to feel the same excitement you did for Christmas Day as a chid. Before dad died I was bouncing off the walls for days in the run-up to a flight to LA and once on board I would spend the whole flight transfixed to Sky Maps watching the little plane icon inch impossibly slowly across the globe for 11 or so hours.

But it's different now, there is no dad waiting for us in Arrivals. On our last phone call before flying I'd always whisper to him to hide so that we could find him, and he would, tucked away behind a stand, kneeling behind a pile of suitcases belonging to other travellers, or sitting at the end of a bench with a newspaper covering his face waiting to be discovered. Wisps of his tightly coiled white hair poking out normally gave him away first. I loved this game, but now as I am older I can understand why mum found this stunt incredibly annoying. I keep telling myself that despite dad not being there physically in person as I step off the plane and out of the immigration hall, he *is* there, in Los Angeles that is, but now I must negotiate arriving by myself, remember the memories but not mourn for them. Now, when the wide electric double doors swing open to reveal the arrivals hall I feel as though I am stepping out of my past and into my future.

We couldn't keep the apartment in Los Angeles and as dad had gone I realised I'd lost my home as well. Knowing Los Angeles would always be a part of my life and city I would return to, the thought of no longer being able to land at LAX and 'go home' was an extremely destabilising feeling and for months I had recurring nightmares of being stranded in Los Angeles or arriving with my suitcases trying to no avail to get into the building that was once home.

As well as a physical structure or built urban environment, place is imbued with symbolic, cultural and psychological meaning, my home in Los Angeles was a place of nurture and excitement, rituals and routine, all of which had been wiped away. It seemed to be the definition of a clean slate. We had two months to move out of the apartment following dad's death and so every day was spent sorting and compartmentalising and arranging shipping - in this time the notion of home was a very transitionary state. Going back to the flat after dad had died felt very strange. Though it was our base too, it was primarily his space, his home, with belongings he'd collected independently from mum or my brother and I and personal items like paperwork and his writings. I no longer felt like I was at home, I felt like we were invading his personal space and suddenly the walls and carpets and tiles and Los Angeles felt more like just buildings and palm trees and traffic.

A month or so after moving out of the apartment the shipment had arrived in Southampton and was on its way to our house in the Cotswolds. My grandma, aunt and uncle had come over to help us unpack it and there was a buzz of excitement in the air, although it wasn't really exciting at all. It wasn't a positive reason why the items were being moved, they shouldn't be here, they should still be in Los Angeles in dad's apartment with him pottering around them and using them and me seeing them behind him on Skype. I shouldn't be helping the movers carry them through the front door covered in cardboard and bubble wrap. I remember that day being absolutely exhausting, not just from the physical effort of heaving items around, but the emotional chaos of it all.

We shipped furniture, paintings and décor that meant the most to us and so I am glad that we have them in England but they don't belong here. The huge vintage French film poster that now hangs in the hallway is supposed to still be above the dining room table where I'd still be able to look at it every morning as I ate my waffles, or smile at it knowing I was home on the evening we'd arrive back in Los Angeles.

The little statues and ornaments that were once gathered together on the mantelpiece to the right of the television that I used to look up at during advert breaks, or remember being hurtled towards us in an earthquake, are now dotted around the house in England. I no longer turn off the Chinese lamp by reaching past the window where I'd feel the soft heat of Los Angeles evening sun and hear the hum of the crickets. It now sits on a bookcase.

In some ways, I feel that dad is with us in England through his possessions, that his personality lives on because these are the pieces he chose: the artwork he really liked and connected with; the photographs that reflect his upbringing in New York; his books, some signed personally to him; his violin. I would prefer having such belongings as opposed to having given them away and though they look good on the walls or on the mantelpiece or dresser, to me they are fundamentally out of place. The meaning and memories I have with them are intertwined with them being placed in Los Angeles.

There is a saying that your house is 'ego' and if this notion is true, then it is no wonder I feel as though I have lost a part of myself following the loss of my home. In a way, your house is a mirror of yourself, your personal feelings, emotions and growth as well as your relationship with those who live in the house with you, and those who do not. Home fosters a sense of self in physical and psychological ways. Time (past and present), place, and material possessions are vehicles for constructing social identities, social traditions and your place in communities. Identity persisted through place further defines who you are, so when that place changes you begin to redefine your identity.

THE 'GLOW-UP' TO 'GROW-UP' - AN IDENTITY CRISIS

Identity Crisis

Before dad became ill many of my thoughts were occupied with my

appearance. What was coming in my Birchbox that month; could I really justify *another* bowl of pasta that week; the flurry of excitement that it was a Tuesday so I could pick up my copy of *Stylist* magazine outside the tube station for my journey home; revisiting my internet search history of best hair curlers for thick hair; or did that skirt make me look dumpy if I wore it with flats rather than shoes with a bit of a heel? All of these material items and thoughts were contributing to my 'glow-up', an (important) event which social media and popular magazines define as when your appearance and/or confidence transform positively over a period of time.

Following dad's death I stopped caring about my appearance, that's not to say I let myself go or lacked any effort in putting an outfit together, but it suddenly didn't matter as much, I didn't care. I'd go out in my glasses rather than contact lenses, I didn't bother with winged eyeliner or taming my frizzy fly-away hair. It just didn't seem important, I had seen what was important and to use a cliché myself, life is too short.

In the two months that turned my world upside down I felt that I had matured by ten years. My perspective and opinions on things had changed, what I wanted for my future became clearer and more urgent, my priorities were reshuffled and some forgotten, and I felt a strong desire to settle down and crave stability, create something that I could control after these times where I wasn't in control of anything and everything in my life had crumbled around me.

Even out with friends I found that I couldn't join in with frivolous conversations or gossip. I would have gleefully joined in before but now I just didn't care, and mostly I just didn't have the energy. I was content to sit quietly, half of my mind present, half of my mind sat in the hospital rooms, watching my friends have fun together, something that I, for a while, felt could never be part of again.

94

The best analogy I came up with when trying to explain this feeling of distance and separation to my friends is imagining I am a little bug at the bottom of a big metal bucket. I can see the light at the top above me but I can't get to it, I'm stuck, enclosed at the bottom watching the world go on above and around me. I can see it, but I can't experience it, I can't laugh like I used to, how can I? I wasn't happy. How could anyone else understand that beneath my face, heavy with extra layers of makeup so you can't see how pale I am, eyes heavy with under-eye concealer and extra mascara to make my eyes pop and my purple eye bags less visible, I'm not there, I'm smiling because I can see everyone else is, but I don't really know what we're talking about and I certainly can't feel it. Of course, my friends likely did know all of this, but you feel so isolated in your grief it's hard to see that.

I guess part of my identity crisis was in the form of mourning my past and stepping into my present, my more mature self. Through caring for dad as you would a young child, negotiating countless doctors' appointments and absorbing their notes, trying to understand them before relaying them to wider family members, witnessing a parent deteriorate before your eyes and witnessing their moment of death makes you grow up fast.

I felt ill-prepared at my age and/or my stage of life, I'd never really had a pet to care for other than a hamster that provided fleeting joy for two years before dying, and I don't have any children so I wasn't ready to step into such an important caring role. I wasn't ready for the role reversal between parent and child, I thought that wasn't supposed to happen until I was at least 40 with a family of my own. This is where I struggled to find guidance and support whilst looking for bereavement books. Most writers were at least ten or 15 years older than me and most with practice of caring for their own children.

I grieve for dad but I also grieve for me, like the saying, 'grieve for those left behind'. I grieve for the future experiences with dad I have been robbed of. I was 24 when dad died, 25 at the time of writing this book and though 25 is technically 'adult' age, I don't feel like a fully-fledged adult, I've left the nest but its safety net is wide and I'm still within it. Whether subconsciously or consciously, I still need my parents' care, emotional and financial support, and just knowing they're there when I need them. I need that from both of them because that is how my life had always been. I'm not used to one half being gone, which in turn has caused the readjustment and reorganization of family roles and relationships.

Though independent, it is an adjustment to now see mum as an individual rather than as a collective 'parent'. She is only mum now, not mum and dad, not one half of '*we* are your *parents*'. Birthday cards are solely signed by her now, there's no 'and dad'. I remember opening my 25th birthday card with apprehension not knowing how mum had decided to sign off. Was it weird to still write 'love from mum and dad'? She wrote 'love from mum', it stung and the pain was sharp and stabbing, she might as well have written 'love from *just* mum' to really rub it in, but I'm sure I would have felt the same had she written the card from both of them, she wouldn't have been able to win in this situation. For a while I toyed with the idea of which way I would have preferred and couldn't come to a conclusion.

Record scratch *freeze frame* 'yup, that's me, you're probably wondering how I got here'* – a defeatist line from the film *The Emperor's New Groove*, a childhood favourite of mine and therefore a quote that came flooding to me at a time when I found myself wallowing in self-pity and wondering how I ended up in the circumstance that I am in. I don't recognise this life, it isn't mine because it is not supposed to happen to me, so I don't recognise me. I look at photographs of myself from recent years before dad died and look at my face thinking, 'you poor girl, you have no idea what is about to happen to your life', and then I think, but what if I had been warned, how would I have changed, what would I have done differently? I don't know.

For a while I avoided mirrors, I couldn't face (excuse the pun) my reflection. Looking at myself in the mirror I can see that my protective bubble of life has gone, cancer popped it. I don't feel like the same person, I feel sorry for my reflection, I try and smile at her, a reassuring gaze or an attempt to bring back the girl who didn't carry the heaviness of grief and depression over her like a hooded cape. She doesn't smile back, she blinks feebly, I think her pale skin is paler and her face is sallower. She looks back at me in a way that says, 'don't pity me' but really screams that she's crying inside. This is when I realised I was having an identity crisis. Looking in the mirror and not recognising myself. Closing my eyes and conjuring up who I think I am, Rose wasn't there anymore, I couldn't reach her. I'm not the girl who loses her dad at 24. I'm not the girl whose family has been turned upside down by cancer, but it seems now that I am.

At the same time, something else in me had changed, with almost a new-found confidence despite crumbling inside. Ironically I felt confident and untouchable, the worst thing that could happen had happened so what could be so bad now? I wore my bereaved identity like a shield that enveloped me. I inwardly willed people (men) to tell me to 'smile love' as they so often enjoy doing, so I could shoot them down and pour out my anger and emotions at them.

Once, a man made the mistake of telling my mum to *'cheer up, its New Year's'* in a checkout queue at a food shop in Los Angeles. He was met with a stern glare from my mum and yet he persisted, *'come on, it's New Year's, be happy'* he advised. I wished I were turtle so I'd be able to retreat into my shell and hide from what I knew was coming. Amongst other choice words, mum's reply was along the lines of *'I have nothing to be happy for, my husband is dying of lung cancer, lymphoma and double kidney failure so don't f*cking tell me to be happy'*. To be fair, he deserved it. It is never OK to try and coax a woman into smiling for you. Mum suggested he tell the men in the queue to smile as well as they began to unpack their shopping onto the cashier conveyor belt…that well-known ear-to-ear grin inducing activity.

Being bereaved almost felt like an excuse to cry or be vulnerable and nothing anyone would say to me would make me feel worse. I became a

98

pro at a 'French exit' – slipping away undetected, knowing that people would understand why I'd left and not call me out for it. Once I had realised this I felt much freer. Before, I had felt too anxious to go out in case I couldn't leave and would be suffocating with the weight of grief in public.

Other 'things' have changed too in my life. All of which I hadn't anticipated before this happened but hit me quite hard. For example, having to tick the 'yes' box or answer 'yes' to a doctor asking if anyone in your immediate family has cancer, having to say, *'yes, my dad'*, and then a slight awkward pause before they try to find out what cancer and what their fate was. I remember the first time this happened it really catching me off-guard and setting off my emotions for the rest of the day.

Another 'new thing' in my life is negotiating language and tenses and carefully crafting answers so as not to upset myself - or make the other person feel uncomfortable - have become a norm. The use of the term 'parents' has unfortunately been retired as it is no longer quite accurate and I find saying parent as a singular too weird in a sentence. I cringe when friends accidentally say, *'how are your parents?'* or *'say hi to your parents from me!'*. It's just a bit cutting. I never really know how to answer questions like *'where do your parents live?'* or *'what do your parents do?'*. I can say *'my mum is blah blah blah'* but then it comes to dad and deciding which tense to use is a real mental battle.

I first came across this hurdle when 'getting to know' an AirBnB guest staying at my boyfriend's flat. My tongue fumbled around the consonants needed for past and present tense words in my mouth as she sat opposite me eagerly slurping down her homemade pho and me forcefully dipping a fish finger into a dippy egg…my mind not in a well-enough state at the time to recognise that was a bizarre mix of food for dinner.

If I use present tense, 'dad does/is blah blah blah' it somehow feels wrong and I risk being asked follow-up questions, yet saying 'dad was a blah blah blah' is either too final, or I fear people will think he has retired or has become too lazy to work, which I feel is a betrayal of dad's identity - his work was so much a part of him. Calling his work to tell them he would not be returning was one of the hardest things mum has had to do, and seeing dad's reaction was one of the hardest things I have had to witness. I think it was at that point he felt his identity slip away and began to realise the seriousness of his situation.

I also found I had a sudden intense interest in how the human body works and how cancer works and how cancer treatments work. I needed to know everything and spent a long time consulting Google and talking to doctors. Perhaps this was in desperation to try and garner a deeper understanding of what was happening, which may in turn have made me feel slightly more in control. I often wondered whether if I were still in school and not as squeamish as I am whether this event would have influenced me to study medicine.

I also wondered whether my successes were now framed in my circumstance. Were people only happy for me because of what I'd been through? Have I only done well because of everything that's happened or would this still be a good achievement? I once announced some good news relating to my PhD on Facebook and was met with many more likes and comments than what I normally received, and though very flattered and grateful, I always wondered whether they would have meant it before. Do people feel like they need to be kinder to me? I definitely received more words of support from a wider audience. I didn't want pity but in truth it was all very warming to read, perhaps my current emotional health had made me cynical.

My emotions and outlook on life had inevitably shifted. My life is forever changed, I won't get over it, things will never go back to how they were. *This is my new normal.* I will adapt my life to my new circumstance, grief and longing for my dad will intertwine itself with every element of my life, forever woven through the future that awaits me, and I hope in time this will offer peace and comfort more than it offers raw, painful emotion.

Maybe it is how I will see my dad again, see him in my head as I face difficult situations, feel his presence at times when I need support, see him grinning when I'm achieving my goals, see him smiling at me through the eyes of my future children. Though invisible to my eye, I can see him in my pretend world, I won't be alone, he will keep me company when I need it. I will feel his fingers scratching my back like he used to, and I'll see him roll his eyes at me after I roll mine at him.

My plans for my future had completely changed, not just in relation to dad not being there, but in relation to my priorities and what I felt was important. I wanted to be settled and stable, I'd rather be cosy with a cup

101

of tea or a glass of wine in a (nice) pub or on the sofa on a weekend than avoiding Jägerbombs and cheap tequila shots at clubs. I wanted my future to be set in stone. I pictured myself knelt in front of a Victorian dolls house mastering exactly what I wanted everyone to do - I needed to be in control of something. I restrained myself from designing my life on The Sims, I thought it would probably be more detrimental to my mental health if I began to live in fantasy Sim land more than the present.

Daily I came across social situations which reinforced the fact my world had stopped but nobody else's had and this was isolating, frustrating and lonely. I regrettably felt anger towards those close to me who were getting on with their day-to-day lives and going out and having fun or not checking in on me at the exact moment I needed it most. Because for them, it's an inconceivable thought, your parents are immortal.

Self-care

I am not religious and I don't get thrills from exercise, not that the two are the same, but they are comparable in the sense that people seek and take comfort from them. For me, neither had anything to offer. As the days dragged into nights and back into days and back into nights, as I slept less and less, as any semblance of a routine washed away and no joy visited my mind or body I knew I had to get on top of self-care.

Self-care is extremely easy to overlook during bereavement. Whilst someone is dying it feels selfish to think about yourself and your own needs, and once the person has died you feel that most things such as putting on a hydrating facemask or cooking a lovely meal is totally mundane. But it is so important! You have to be selfish and put yourself first. It took me a while to realise this but I am so glad that I did, and it helped me in ways that I believe went beyond the 'placebo effect'.

Disclaimer: I'm not a vegan, I'm not about to try a Keto diet or anything like that, I find my thoughts and especially grief are too distracting for yoga and I haven't run in about 10 years when I'd drag myself around my school's cross-country track purely out of fear of detention because I was predominantly a teacher's pet. I just really don't find joy in exercise other than dance so I also do not have a gym membership or the desire to go and get one. So when it came to self-care I really had to think hard about what I could do to make myself feel better, mainly wanting to avoid fads and on-trend activities and knowing that dragging myself to the gym would require a lot more mental energy and determination than I was prepared to give away. I realised it didn't have to be anything new; I didn't need to turn into a bodybuilder. I just had to think back to what used to make me feel happy, what made me feel like Rose. I did some mental brainstorming:

☐ What made me feel saner?

☐ What made me feel mentally healthier?

☐ What made me feel physically healthier?

☐ What did I really enjoy before all of this? Would doing that again now help, or at this time would it increase stress and anxiety?

☐ What would make me feel rooted and calm?

☐ What would make me feel stable amongst the shattering of life around me?

A kitten was the most obvious and pressing choice but alas, my circumstance dictated that now was not the right time. Perhaps it will be in August…for my birthday. I whittled my thoughts down to a few main categories – writing, dancing, eating, pampering.

I really recommend jotting down thoughts on how you are feeling. I actually never did this on paper even though I bought a really lovely leather-bound notepad from John Lewis, something which took me an arduously long time to pick out because it had to be just right, despite ending up never opening the seal…yet.

104

Instead I recorded things on the Notes app on my phone and on a Google Doc so I could add to it on the move when I needed to release thoughts building in my head. I found this really helped clear some headspace too. Though I abhor the phrase, 'time will heal' looking back over the months, and from being able to reflect upon emotions in this book, it is interesting be able to read the thoughts and emotions I was experiencing and see the patterns they have taken and what has changed over time. For example, my anger is now less fuelled in rage and resentment, but rather the feeling of unfairness and pity for my dad and myself. Though still an encircling part of my day, the times I fully get upset have lessened, yet when they do come they feel a lot more severe, I cry harder and my thoughts go deeper and it is tougher to climb out of the sorrow.

Dance has always been a huge part of my life. I started ballet at the age of three and did it until I was 18 and moved away to university. As I got older the length of my lessons increased and I attended classes three or fours times a week. Ballet was totally a part of me, the way I held myself, the way I walked, the discipline it instilled within me, my musicality and movement. Whilst still living at home it was very rare if I walked normally into another room without executing a grand jeté or posé turns down the hall. I couldn't bend to pick something up without my leg involuntarily raising into a penché arabesque or stand without practising my relevés.

I bet a day didn't go by without mum yelling something along the lines of *'oh will you stay still!'* whilst trying to talk to me. As a result, ballet not only shaped my body, but also my mind. My body and mind felt healthy when I did ballet but this was something I didn't realise until I moved away to university in 2011 and stopped going due to cost of lessons. Fast forward seven years to 2018, I knew I had to do something physical to alleviate stiffness and hopefully experience those happy endorphins everyone told me I would if I just did a bit of exercise. I found an adult ballet class in London and paid upfront for a block of six lessons: no matter how much I may enjoy it, I knew I had to pay upfront in order to motivate myself to go each week.

I remember so vividly the first lesson I went to and how the act of packing my leotard, tights and ballet shoes into my bag slapped me in the face with nostalgia. Something I had done hundreds and hundreds of times before, but always in the context of dad being alive. Even though ballet was 'mum's thing', having gone to the Royal Ballet School, dad always asked me how my lesson was that day, it was part of our daily debrief.

I remembered being much younger and skipping off to class knowing that by the time I came out, Los Angeles would be awake and dad would soon be calling. I nearly bailed, thinking if I can't hold myself together now whilst perching on the end of the bed idly piling some things into my bag, how would I cope whilst there? But I did go and I loved it and I kept going back! Having trained for so many years I knew how to focus my attention on the music and ensure I was properly engaging the right muscles and my slight competitive streak of wanting to be the best came out and motivated me further so during the lesson I was totally absorbed in something other than grief. That feeling stayed for a couple of hours after the lesson, enough time for me to get home and relax and get into bed, and the feeling of my body being stretched and worked was a refreshing feeling to wake up to the following morning.

Growing up and for a couple of years living in London I had ballroom, latin and flamenco dance lessons which I loved, they were so much fun and a great workout. Though the thought of ballet class one night a week, and then potentially two other dance classes, was a bit overwhelming in my current headspace of mild agoraphobia I found going over previously learnt routines in my head and putting them into practice was a good stress-reliever.

Even when I was really sad, if I could force myself up off the sofa and cha-cha through the flat it would actually make me smile. It was nice knowing that I didn't have to throw myself into a brand new activity to try and feel better, I could return to an old favourite and feel joy whilst doing it and also encouraging the feeling of already being pretty good at it rather than starting from scratch and the frustrations that could come with that.

Eating. I love to eat and I used to pride myself on the huge portion sizes I could consume and not feel full. Luckily my best friend is very similar and so no judgments passed. The amount of times we'd be out for food and a waiter would look at us sceptically and warn us that we'd ordered quite a lot of food, only to return a while later to find the bowls scraped clean…we're looking at you, Dishoom. We've also wondered when is enough cheese in a mac and cheese ever enough, quantity wise and type?

And is it really that bad that we'd finish a whole bag of Sensations crisps just in the process of making it?

You can only imagine my sorrow and - honestly - fear in the sense of what is the point of living, when I realised that a symptom of grief I was experiencing was not only lack of appetite but lack of interest in food (mega sob). Disclaimer: luckily this lack of interest only lasted a short while although lack of appetite and a change in taste buds persisted, but at least I could get excited about a meal whether I wanted it or not.

During my stint in Atlanta whilst dad was there in hospital and then back in LA my diet consisted pretty much wholly of avocados, lentils, tomatoes, rye bread, bagel and cream cheese (the only palatable thing I could find in the hospital cafés), corn-chips, wine and gin, and so by default, limes too. I really can't remember eating anything else between November 2017 and February 22nd 2018 when I returned to England to 'get on with my life'.

I've always had a bit of a weird relationship with food anyway, despite never really holding myself back from eating what I want I still felt pangs of guilt, unattractiveness and general unhealthiness if it had been a couple of days since I'd not eaten a responsible adult quantity of vegetables or if I'd had pasta for more meals than not in a week. I found food was very important in my self-care routine and massively affected (probably more than it should have) how I felt for the rest of the day, specifically in relation to my grief.

Although I can definitely remember the way a day would drag at school if I'd discovered poached salmon, green beans and new potatoes were on the menu for dinner. Back in London I tried to eat responsibly, I'd never really eaten badly anyway and always had a balanced diet and 'treats' such as a solo wine gum or a couple of celery sticks to snack on growing up, but it seemed more than ever food, type and amount, was crucial to my wellbeing.

I'm more of a starter over dessert kind of gal but I found if I had too little sugar I'd turn into a shaking, tired, lethargic crying mess. A glass of orange juice, fizzy Haribo and spoonfuls of peanut butter straight from the jar usually solved this although it was always in quite a bingeful way. I had to learn to not let myself get to this stage and feed myself when needed, even if eating was the last thing I felt like doing. If I ate too much cheese or pasta (my total faves) I'd find the satisfaction was very temporary and would be taken over with guilt, which in turn would enhance my anxiety.

On the flipside, if I ate lots of fruit, vegetables and healthy snacks I would feel positive overall, yet the saintly halo over my head, or imagine the green diamond above a Sim, would loose its vibrancy as they emphasised my feeling of longing (for carbs or a delicious homemade carbonara), which in turn just made me sad and go in search of a piece of chocolate. Two firm faves for mood-boosting are grapes: sweet, refreshing, a bit 'treat-like', natural sugar etc; and salted nuts: yummy, filling, good for you in moderation, easy to snack on, not nauseating.

I've probably consumed the most alcohol, since learning of dad's diagnosis, than at any other time in my life, even first year of university.

However this was only ever wine/prosecco/champagne or gin and never enough to get drunk or to completely numb the pain. At five foot tall I am a massive lightweight and, like most people I'm sure, I dislike the feeling of a hangover. I just drank enough to enjoy the taste (I don't drink if I don't like what it tastes like) and feel a slight buzz and to relax me, never enough to tip me over the edge into a wine-drunk blubbering mess, which I genuinely feared.

I never really used alcohol as a coping mechanism and was very conscious of all the pamphlets detailing how grief can turn to alcohol addiction and dependency, or worse, to drugs. I shall refrain from going into my personal feelings towards every meal I ate for the first year, but basically the crux of the matter is, a balanced diet was extremely important, not just for general health, but balancing out my mental equilibrium.

Pampering, my fourth self-care category, encompasses several genres covering cleanliness and routine. Obviously I enjoy being a clean person, absolute hurl when a smelly person gets on a bus or tube and you're trapped in their air until the doors open again at the next stop. But not only did I shower for reasons such as being a conscientious human being out and about amongst London society, I found showering always made me feel mentally and physically better. A good shower stint would completely expel any emotions I was feeling pre-shower and by the time I got out I had usually managed to distract myself with a new thought such as a PhD fret, a mental note of needing to wash the bathmat or something profound like what is the meaning of life? The steam from the shower helped to unblock sinuses, stop a runny nose, help a tension headache and clear the tears welling beneath the surface of my eyes. If I

110

relaxed into it properly the heat of the water helped to alleviate aches and pains.

Other than general pampering like putting makeup on, doing a facemask from time to time, brushing my hair properly and maybe trying out a new shampoo (the thrills!), there were other honestly quite inconsequential small things that I found had a big impact on my mood. Part of this was routine, which helped to alleviate my sense of being unsettled and in turn helped me sleep better. I tried to go to bed at the same time each night and wind down for an hour or so beforehand, this helped me structure my evening and eliminate sitting on the sofa for too long ruminating over something someone said in the hospital or something I won't be able to do with dad anymore.

Post shower I'd all-over-moisturise, obviously good for my skin and it felt like an adult thing to do, and apply a night cream to my face. It just felt like one step up from a normal moisturiser, this was specifically designed for night, thank you jojoba oil and boreal algae. Once applied and absorbed for a few minutes I'd then dab a few drops of rose oil onto my cheek bones. Honestly I don't really know what this did, the vial stated hydration and revitalisation, but for me the main benefits were that it didn't feel greasy on my skin and it smelled really pleasant which was a bonus for going to sleep.

Next I would apply lavender oil onto my wrists. This helps to alleviate stress and tension headaches, and again smelled lovely. For good measure I also sprayed lavender spray along my pillow and on top of the duvet to help induce sleep. It felt very 'pampery' and luxurious and always made me smile right before bed and calm me even if I'd had a tough day.

From August 2018, I embarked on the fieldwork component on my PhD. The assigned 12-month stint 'in the field' was to conduct in-depth and in-person research pertaining to my project. During this time away from my boyfriend, friends and family in London I was inevitably on my own, having left my support network and was now eight hours behind them and this took a massive mental toll on me. I didn't actually realise how much it had affected me until I returned home for Christmas, in the same way people say 'you don't know what you had 'till it's gone', I felt I didn't realise how unhappy I'd been until I felt how happy I was being back.

Being in Los Angeles with the time difference meant not only was I physically by myself (unless I went out and made friends), I was also alone in a communicative sense from 3pm LA time/11pm UK time - until about 11pm LA/7am UK time when my friends would be beginning to wake for work. Selfishly I'd be thrilled if any of them, especially my boyfriend, woke up in the middle of the night or couldn't sleep. The flutter of excitement I'd get when my phone would buzz at 8pm LA time meaning someone was awake at five in the morning. A close friend had gone travelling in Thailand and it took a couple of months for us to realise that our 15-hour time difference, (mind-blown) was super beneficial to both of us. As our friends in England were heading off to bed, she'd be just waking up and it would be mid-afternoon for me, then by the time I had gone to bed and woke up around 7ish, it would be late evening for her and we could have a little debrief about her day. It was mutually extremely beneficial for both of us.

I realised early on that if I were going to get through it without the support network I had grown reliant upon, I had to be my own support and look after myself. Something integral to this was forming a routine. I made myself get up by a certain time, set myself a bed time, or at least a time to be in bed by, whether that meant I then read or watched something on Netflix, and times through the day to check in with myself like a work progress report.

A routine gave me something to focus on and work towards and a structure to my day which was so important, I think especially because that's the way my personality operates. I made my three meals a focal point of my day so that not only did I ensure I was eating and not skipping meals and making something healthy, it helped to break up my days into what seemed like manageable chunks.

I even toyed with the concept of intermittent fasting, the practice of only allowing yourself to eat within a small window of the day such as between 11am and 4pm and then fasting for 19 hours (gawp) with the aim of losing weight. This was not my aim and I still ate as much as I would do normally and 'fasted' for 15 hours instead, but it meant I didn't get hungry between meals so didn't snack – something I found I was previously doing a lot due to boredom. My mood was boosted because I didn't have to finish lunch and feel sorrow that I wasn't having dinner for another seven hours for example, and by having an earlier dinner I went to bed feeling less bloated and full and consequently slept better.

By confining my meals to a shorter time period I also felt more alert and energised. My day would look something like: wake at 7ish, lie in bed and reply to any messages I'd received overnight, maybe read for a while and then get up and shower. I'd have my cup of tea and some water (I didn't count liquids) around 9ish and then get on with work. By 10:30/11am I was usually pretty hungry for breakfast. Lunch would come at about 2pm and then dinner by 5:30/6. I'm very aware that this food routine was only really doable because of my circumstance of being by myself and no real time pressures like having to get to work by 9am and not getting home until gone 7:30pm.

In general I really dislike being by myself. It's not that I can't entertain myself, get bored easily or haven't got things to be getting on with (#PhD), I just prefer being around other people, and since everything that happened with dad I fear being alone means no distraction from sad thoughts. This is something I really had to overcome in the field so as not to drive myself insane, or my boyfriend insane by requesting Skype calls for hours on end.

For company/a bit of noise I started to listen to podcasts and very quickly found them very addictive. I listened to them so much I started to believe that the hosts were my friends having a chat with me through my phone (I don't mean that as sad as it sounds). Not only did they provide a bit of silence-eliminating comfort but they were also engaging topics and gave me new ideas to think about and discuss with people so also proved to be a good respite from constant uni work. When I worked I listened to classical music playlists a lot of which I recognised from ballets and

114

operas. I've never been able to concentrate on work fully if the TV has been on in the background or if songs with lyrics have been playing because I find myself either singing along or accidentally writing down the lyrics, whereas classical music filled the silence and I found it strangely motivating. It's not like it was crazily energising music you might hear in a spin class but it was captivating which encouraged me to stay focused and press through with my work.

The first fieldwork stint was four months and mentally getting through that time came down a lot of the time to mind tricks with calendars like congratulating myself for every month that passed, or picking out mid-month targets to get to. I'm so excited to come home…in three months time… was better for me to look forward to getting back, even with 90 days remaining, than it was for me to accept that that was actually quite a long time and there was no point in getting excited. In a way I definitely was counting down the days and wishing the time away but I couldn't help it and given my circumstance, I don't feel guilty about it.

THE LESSER-SPOTTED-ACCIDENTAL-INSULTER
AND THE HERD OF NON-BEREAVED

Clichés

If you're bereaved, you've come across them. The mean-weller but opposite-effecter who come out with dreaded statements of advice and support such as, *'you'll get over it'*, variations of the cliché *'time will heal'* / *'it will get better with time'*, and other enraging statements like *'well you look fine now'* or *'you haven't cried in a while'*. The most important thing to remember is that these statements are said by people who mean well - and not with

117

malice - though, crucially, make you (or maybe just me) feel shit, cringe and feel my fingers begin to curl into tight little fists. *They're just trying to help'* is something I'd tell myself over and over because frankly I became so 'over everything' in the months following dad's death that some acquaintances were culled from my life as I only had time for people who truly cared about me. The thought of hanging out with people I wasn't that fussed about suddenly seemed and became a truly ridiculous use of time, mental and emotional effort.

Clichés I heard a lot and hated were sayings along the lines of, '*it is times like these that bring people closer together*'. This is definitely not always the case. Families can be torn apart by the death of a loved one if those involved cope with grief differently which, due to personality clashes, arguments, resentments and intense friction can arise. If you are experiencing this, you are not alone, this is not unusual, and you have not failed whom you are all grieving for. I hated questions like '*how are you all coping?*' and thus the unavoidable collective 'we'. Every time I would hear someone ask mum on the phone this question I would cringe inside, resenting a sentence along the lines of 'we are fine' coming out of her mouth. We were certainly not fine.

At the same time, I hated being asked the same question and then have to come up with an answer about how mum was coping or how my brother was coping. In truth I had no idea, just as much as they had no idea how I was coping, because its intensely personal and private and just because my brother for example hadn't seen me cry for a while, doesn't mean that I'm fine, it doesn't mean I do not cry. But, we were all very

118

'keep calm and carry on' British about it all, and thus 'we are all fine', and people accepted that as an answer, which when you think about it, is completely absurd on all accounts.

Re-negotiating Friendships and Support

I have been extremely lucky when it comes to support from my friends but one of the first things I noticed was how differently friends reacted to the news and how they supported me going forward. From all-day messaging (my best friend and I have on-going message chats all day long, leaving each other's houses or restaurant dates with the line 'message you in two mins' rather than 'bye'), to phone calls, cards, to flowers in the immediate time following the diagnosis and also the death, and friends putting me in touch with others they knew in similar circumstances. Despite feeling totally supported by some, I couldn't help by feel let down by others and found myself having to recall the phrase 'you'll always be disappointed when you expect people to act as you would' often. This was difficult to come to terms with and wondered whether I was perhaps being too needy or expecting too much and I hope anyone reading experiencing the same renegotiation of social life finds comfort in knowing this is normal.

Dealing with the loss of friends, not that they had died, but the gravity of which I had held their relationship to me, changed, and those who I previously had believed were close friends didn't reach out or offer messages of support or thought as the months went by, whilst others who previously were less close came through and offered me a lot of support.

Though it feels like some are being 'bad friends' or make you question, 'are we even friends anymore?' I had to keep telling myself that as they haven't experienced grief, they may be worried they'll say the wrong thing or upset me more, or plainly not know what to say, or don't know the level of support I required, not just in the days after the death, but in the weeks and months following.

Their world has continued, unchanged. People will surprise you and friendships change in response to that, and for me, this has in some ways been a silver lining, making my bond with certain friends stronger and deeper. I talk to some people more than before and take the place of someone who had previously been in that spot. (Think about back in the day on BEBO when you'd re-evaluate the positions on your Top 16 Friends list, a very important end-of-the-week job, potentially mid-week if something had really gone awry in the playground).

Though I had the unwavering support of my boyfriend and certain friends, at times I was still left feeling lonely and isolated because those who had not experienced a death could only understand to an extent, and a deeper level became abstract and I risked hearing them come out with a cliché which I desperately didn't want to hear. At the same time I felt like I had joined a club – a club of bereaved 20-somethings, not one I would voluntarily have joined but one I was firmly in and was thankful for the network. It wasn't so much the case that my friendships with those who had also lost a parent became 'better', but instead deeper, we had moved onto a different level of understanding from everyone else, almost like a shared memory, and equally friendships with new bereaved sons and daughters blossomed more quickly than normal.

I found with those who understood we could laugh about death without it being macabre and converse seriously with each other about the things we had witnessed and the intense feelings we possessed, the ability to state 'what's the point?' without someone thinking you're suicidal. About six months after dad's death I was fortunate enough to be connected to a group of young women who had also unfortunately lost parents and were looking for others to talk to and connect with on the deeper level, to have the conversations we couldn't have with friends and maybe not even family.

One summer evening in late July I was sat in a pub in East London waiting for the group to arrive. The organiser had rented part of the establishment for our meet-up and frequently the bar staff nervously glanced over to those of us who were early, waiting to see when we'd be ready to go to our allotted space, pity and awkwardness in their gazes. I'd look at any young woman entering the pub to see if they fit the bereaved criteria and would be joining us: do they look a bit puffy around the eyes, weary, or drained of sleep? Is that waterproof mascara? Is that the slightly glossed-over look in their eyes that suggests they're there but not present?

One of the hardest things to come to terms with mentally was accepting that no one else's world had stopped. Just mine. I couldn't be mad at my friends for still being cheery, or suggesting nights out or throwing house parties, or being at work when I desperately needed to phone them, or for them to be enjoying a day out with their dads on Father's Day when I needed them. I had to be patient and I had to make myself understand. But it's hard; in those times of grief you are irrational and selfish.

Dispelling thoughts such as 'so-and-so hasn't messaged me in two days', or 'this person started talking about her dad in front of me' from my mind was hard, and I repeatedly told myself it doesn't mean they're no longer my friends or that they've acted maliciously.

I also never knew how to answer questions such as *'how're you doing?'* if I was out and about. I still don't. Do I reply with the usual 'yeah fine' or 'good thanks, how are you?' or do I go deeper and tell them how I'm actually feeling? Is that what they've actually asked me, how I'm *really* doing, or is to tell them about my sleepless night and not being able to get the 'death rattle' noise out of my head a bit too doom and gloom over brunch?

I find it is a constant battle of second-guessing what friends mean and second-guessing how I should respond or act. What if I tell them how I'm feeling and then I don't get invited to things because I'm too sad and might bring the mood down? But what if I smile or laugh too much? Will they think then that I'm fine and no longer check-in with me? That was too much of a risk. I often caught myself justifying how sad I was, or following up a sentence with my true feelings like, *'yeah I had such a fun time yesterday evening, the play was great and we had some drinks afterwards...but you know, I'm still really sad and cry all the time'.*

Negotiating grief with those around you who have not experienced bereavement is essential yet difficult. I found it particularly frustrating when someone I would want to have a discussion with is a better listener, and someone who I wanted to just listen wants to ask questions when you're not in the mood.

It sounds self-centred and like you want to have your cake and eat it too and your friends must all fall in line under your new emotional-need-driven regime, but it's true, you need support and you need it in the way *you* need it and coming to terms with friends not giving you what you want from them is tough to let go. Something that really helped me was reminding myself that I don't need someone to tick all boxes, and I shouldn't expect it. With a large support network, it was like I could pool my resources and in total have my needs met rather than rely on an individual for everything, which wasn't fair on them.

About a year after dad died my boyfriend and I spoke about his experience and the role partners play in the bereavement process. He raised issues to me that I hadn't registered because I was so enveloped in my own feelings. For example, every time I told him how I was feeling, or woke him up crying in the middle of the night, he felt like each time he had to think of something new and comforting to say, despite perhaps being preoccupied with something else, or half asleep at 3am. He described this like being in front of an automatic ball dispenser. Trying to bat my sadness away with new, non-cliché and comforting lines that he was continuously having to create.

He also spoke about second-hand grief and the anxiety and emotional stressors that come with that. For example, not really having an outlet for the grief he was feeling, and not knowing who to turn to for support when supporting me got too much. He described feeling intense sadness watching the person he loves experiencing bereavement, but not feeling like it was his grief or sadness to talk about and so bottling it up.

I understood what he meant as I too have been on the supporting side after an ex-boyfriend's father passed away whilst we were together. I remember that feeling of sadness and hopelessness, knowing I needed to be there but knowing that really very little I did or said was going to take any of their pain away, and knowing that I couldn't talk to them about how I was feeling.

The saying goes, 'grieve for those left behind', but who do those grieving for those who are left behind turn to? This isn't just the case for partners of course, but also for close friends and family members. The emotional toll on those who make up your closest support network should not be underestimated.

A TALE OF TWO CITIES - CULTURE CLASHES AND

LIVESTREAM FUNERALS

There were 11 days between dad's death and his funeral on February

4th 2018, unintentionally but perhaps fittingly, World Cancer Day, although extremely against the Jewish religion. The day after he passed I busied myself by organising the funeral with my mum and beginning the long task of clearing dad's belongings. I went into what I call machine mode, I couldn't stop, adrenaline had filled me like a fully-charged battery and I went about the next few days devoid of emotion, completely numb.

We had the task of emptying dad's home in Los Angeles, deciding what was to be thrown out, what was to be donated to charity and what we'd keep and thus have shipped back to England.

The first arrangement to be made was where dad would be buried. As dad was raised Jewish, cremation (our preferred option), was out of the question and negotiating a funeral that was Jewish, yet accessible to non-religious attendees, including ourselves, became a primary task. I confessed I wouldn't attend my father's funeral if it were to all be in Hebrew and Yiddish rendering me unable to understand what was going on whilst battling inwardly trying to comprehend what had just happened to my life at the same time. With the recommendation of Jewish family members, we located Mount Sinai Memorial Park as dad's final resting place and funeral venue.

Being in the Hollywood Hills prices were extortionate and mum and I found we were out of our depth not only with all the post-death paperwork but also Jewish burial customs. A cheaper option, wall crypts, piqued our interest and I whispered to mum to ask the funeral director on the phone if wall crypts were in keeping with the Jewish faith. He tersely replied, *'yes, this is a Jewish cemetery'* and at that moment it became clear to him that we had no idea what we were talking about.

A couple of days later we were sat around a circular table in a small room at the memorial park awaiting our consultation. The room had the kind of walls you find at conferences that can be pulled back to rearrange room sizes and shapes, I felt this added to the impermanence of life, your temporality on this earth. A man walked in, 'Property Consultant' written

128

across his name-tag... I imagined the process of funeral arrangements were probably quite different in England, simply picking a grave site rather than a weird notion of actually *buying a property* in the Hollywood Hills as they insinuated.

The wall crypt allotted for dad was tucked away: imagine a cul-de-sac of graves, shade sheltering each other as the sun beat down with native Californian plants and trees surrounding them, hummingbirds darting in and out and the soothing trickle of a water fountain filling the otherwise silent air. Dad was on the sixth 'floor' as we called it, not quite the penthouse suite which would have been the seventh tier, but close enough. We affectionately call it his studio apartment in the Hollywood Hills.

The meeting consisted of a lot of paperwork and legal questions, but also queries pertaining to Jewish burial customs. We were told that dad had not been left alone even for a second since he arrived there from the hospital. This is a Jewish custom, we soon learnt, but not soon enough to stop myself from shooting a confused smirk to my mum who under the nervousness and ridiculousness of the situation, (planning a funeral for dad) found herself stifling a laugh. *Shemira:* the religious ritual act of keeping watch over the deceased from the time of death to burial with the aim of offering comfort to the deceased's soul.

According to Jewish tradition, the body is not to be dressed in normal clothes (sorry, burnt orange linen Banana Republic shirt I always thought looked great on him), instead in a plain white garb, either muslin or linen. The man took us to view the *Tachrichim*, letting us choose which we'd prefer dad to be dressed in. He realised showing us was imperative when we sat blinking unknowingly at him when he first spoke the word Tachrichim. He had his work cut out!

I found the most surreal task of all was choosing the casket. We walked into a large room filled with caskets mounted in layers to the four walls. Some were very simple and plain, others were more ornate and made from more expensive and luxurious woods. Physically seeing them sent chills through me and I found it particularly disturbing, although to this day I can't place my finger on exactly why. We chose a simple design and left the room. I can't remember much else from the meeting other than a lot of Jewish-to-English translation and explanations of customs. I guess we didn't know how to feel, whether to shrug off the Jewish burial customs, thinking dad would be laughing at us trying to figure this all out for him, or whether though in life we'd called him 'the Holiday Jew', perhaps in death, this was truly meaningful for him.

We worried in the car on the way home if we'd come across 'too British' about the whole thing, with a 'keep calm and carry on demeanour' rather than a more elaborate American showing of grief we had witnessed. We decided we would have to work on this so as not to come across as uncaring.

Another Jewish custom I hadn't expected and found strange was the lack of flowers. Sending flowers to those left behind is not widely practised in Jewish communities although we didn't find this out until after I Googled it, suspicious of the lack of floral arrangements. The only flowers we received were those sent from non-Jewish friends and family back in England. Jewish mourners sent bagels, challah breads and Jewish cakes and sweet treats which, to be honest, were greatly appreciated.

130

Something I didn't expect to be doing was Googling 'what to expect at a Jewish funeral?, 'Jewish funeral hymns' and 'Jewish burial customs' but not wanting to be left in the dark with it all and being mindful of giving dad the send-off he would want some online research was necessary, it also helped me feel a little more in control. We decided we did not want the service to be a solemn affair and so instead asked those who would be talking to relay happy memories and sentiments, and we chose upbeat music that reminded us most of dad, tunes he would hum or play on his violin, or songs he would sing to us as children or down the phone.

In the days leading up to the funeral I busied myself with outfit picking, a sophisticated black A-line Ted Baker dress with shimmer sewn into it and makeup tutorials, silver smoky eyes and deep purple-red lipstick topped with large sunglasses for the procession from the chapel to the crypt, (very Jackie-O I thought each time I glimpsed my reflection). Perhaps to some trivial, but for me I thought if I'm going to bury my dad, something I never imagined having to do any time soon, I may as well look good doing it, it's what dad would want, and it would be fitting to throw in a bit of Hollywood glamour.

Perhaps having watched all seven seasons of *Pretty Little Liars* had something to do with it, I mean really, how many funerals do high-school girls really go to, I think I counted about ten!

People had often told me, 'you won't remember the funeral, it'll be such a blur', but actually I remember it well. Mum, a choreographer and director, orchestrated the whole affair and it all went strictly to plan. The

131

Cantor carefully weaved Jewish scripture and songs into the service without excluding us, I even found comfort in hearing the *Mourners Kaddish*, a Jewish hymn, I can recall the speeches from family and friends, the sounds of stifled sobs or clear wailing from attendees, although I couldn't once bring myself to look behind me to see who was there.

I recall the thoughts and emotions I felt sitting on the front pew. The inward battle between trying to concentrate, not to cry, not to stare too long at the casket lying in front of me whose contents seemed so surreal and impossible still, thoughts such as is my dress tucked into my knickers each time I had to stand up and sit back down (a lot), is this a good angle…Oh yes, I forgot to say the funeral, in Hollywood fashion, was live streamed. Though quite funny and 'classic LA', it proved very useful for family members who were unable to travel, those of my dad's family dispersed around the US, and my English family back home. It also meant my boyfriend and some friends in England could watch it too which although I'm sure was not gripping Sunday entertainment for them, it was also the Super Bowl, it meant more to me than I can describe. To know I was going through this without them in Los Angeles but had people who cared enough to tune in and watch, and who I could talk about it with, was extremely comforting.

The end of the service was signalled by the instrumental sound of '*bah-da-dum, bah-da-dum, bah-da-dum, bah-da-dum, when a moon hits your eyes like a big pizza pie, that's amore*'. We had chosen Dean Martin's *That's Amore* as the song people would process out to. Dad would always sing this song to us, and it worked as we'd hoped, a split-second of sharp intakes of breath

132

from those in the congregation behind us expecting a slower or solemn classical piece, and then an eruption of laughter and cheer as people recognised the song and could agree it was a perfectly fitting end. Even now, I find it hard not to listen to the song without a smile stretching across my face and my cheeks feeling flushed and warm.

The next part of the funeral was the procession from the chapel to the crypt site further into the memorial park. A chaos of cars, trips to the loo, a quick bite of a cereal bar, missing casket-bearers and bizarreness. Dad would have found it very amusing. We gathered in as close as we could around the crypt whilst dad's casket was placed on a trolley system ready to be elevated into the wall space. Something I had been wondering how it would be done. The Cantor concluded the part of the service here, this part I don't remember well, other than the Jewish practice of ripping your clothes - I believe to symbolise how torn up you are over the death. We politely declined to do this exactly and instead wore little black rosette pins which the Cantor ripped for us. There was some other ripping going on in the congregation but my Ted Baker dress remained intact, phew.

It was then time for dad to be winched up to his space. Two men, gardeners or groundsmen stood on either side of the platform holding the casket in place as the trolley system began to rise. It went incredibly slowly, and it made a ridiculous squeaking noise all the way up before arriving and dad's casket being bumped into place in the wall. Honestly, it was hard not to laugh or imagine the same scene playing out in a British sitcom.

I couldn't help but feel that American funerals were more obtrusive and intrusive than British funerals, or at least ones that I have attended. A lot of people bought plus-ones or their families, even extended family members, many of which had never met dad. I found this particularly unsettling and invasive, like voyeurs of my bad luck on a day-trip to a funeral with a lot of free Jewish deli food on the go. I can't imagine being invited to a funeral and looking forward to going, or even the thought of going as a plus-one.

To me, funerals have always been a solemn occasion, perhaps more of an obligation to go with the whole affair being a bit uncomfortable and awkward for English sensibilities. I looked with disdain at those (predominantly the extras) who had not dressed smartly and instead were in jeans or grubby outfits or chewing gum. Worse still I found were the plus-ones or non-dad acquaintances who also had no idea who the immediate grieving family were. One such woman, whose name I didn't care to remember, abruptly asked, *'who are you?'* whilst not standing long enough for me to answer and instead moving onto a family member she recognised. I hated her. She's on my list.

For me, this was the worst part of the day, it wasn't relaxing, there were people everywhere trying to talk to me, and at me, I couldn't grab anything to eat because I was being pulled in all directions. It was utterly exhausting. I resented those telling me about their loved ones who had died, or other funerals they had been to, or a pet that had died, in that moment I didn't care. Some told me how much dad dying had made them revaluate their life and priorities, whilst others mournfully mentioned life events my dad would no longer be a part of, no one to walk me down the aisle now was a recurring theme which made me sick to my stomach. Not

134

because of the loss, but because it was such a strikingly inappropriate thing to say.

In that afternoon, no one else could possibly have related to how I was feeling and so in my opinion should not have tried. I always had such a caring personality, willingly taking on others' problems to give them a respite, but this time I couldn't. Looking back I know they were either trying to offer words of support and relatedness, or even as a way of talking through their emotions, but for me it wasn't the time. I resented being the shoulder for everyone else to cry on. My waterproof mascara was never tested.

I remember thinking this is what planning a wedding or being at my wedding must feel like; though it was dad's funeral, I was the centre of attention, I had to say hello to everyone, and everyone wanted to talk to me. I remember standing patiently whilst a man whom dad had not seen for probably 20 or more years and who I had never heard of told me why I was called 'Rose'. Something about him going away and dad watering his roses or vice-versa. Something mum said was a false claim.

One family friend said, *'we can talk about this later, for now, let's talk about this dress!'* whilst elaborately raising his arms up and down towards me with a wink. It was refreshing, a semblance of a normal conversation. He was right, we didn't have to talk about dad or death in that moment, we'd have plenty of time to do that later, and we have done in more appropriate settings with a glass of wine, but it was nice to be complimented and have someone say something to me that had nothing to do with a funeral.

I 'hung out' for a while with my dad's most recent assistant who'd I got on well with and had socialised with a few times unconnected to her

135

working with dad. She made me laugh by stating that being in the same place with many of dad's other assistants prior to her had made her feel as though she was in a room with a load of ex's and stood by her assertion that she was queen bee, top assistant. She also told mum that if she has any problems with paperwork, phones, laptops, subscriptions then to get in touch because she probably remembers all the passwords. This was a reassuring lifeline for mum!

The reception had been held at my aunt and uncle's house and after most people had left we opened a bottle of champagne with remaining family members. We wearily left an hour or so later and had an exhausted debrief of the day back at dad's apartment. I don't remember getting into bed or how I felt lying there. The next thing I remember is waking up the following day feeling like the weight of the world had for a moment released me from under its grip. I felt relief that it was over.

A difference to before the funeral was the stark silence that followed, very few people continued to check in with us to see how we were doing. I'm not sure whether I minded or not, as those who did were those we wanted to talk to anyway, but it was just the juxtaposition of everything being manic and happening before the funeral, and then silence, everyone else's lives truly had gone on. The only remaining evidence of the funeral was the cards collected from the service, offers to sit *Shiva* with us, which we declined, not doing so ourselves, and a shiva candle.

The candle was to be lit as soon as we returned from the cemetery and would burn for seven days, the traditional length of the shiva period. I was skeptical that the candle would burn that long, or at least not be

136

'accidentally' blown out, but to my pleasant surprise it lasted the full seven days. In the Jewish faith the candle flame represents the soul reaching upwards and so the soul is aided and comforted for its seven-day journey. Rather unceremoniously we placed ours in one side of the sink. Mum and I don't like leaving a room with a candle burning, let alone going to sleep or leaving the apartment, so the sink seemed like the best option. I can't even go to sleep at night without turning appliances off at the plug, so obviously an overnight dishwasher or washing machine cycle is a no-no.

Dad's Gone Viral...

Dying in the age of social media is a weird one; it was as invasive as it was useful and supportive. For quite a few weeks we had managed to keep dad's deteriorating health off of social media and from being widely known. Very close friends knew the severity of the situation, but others, such as those he was working with, were told he was just having some kidney issues. It wasn't until a friend of dad's wrote a heartfelt plea on Facebook for 'well wishes and prayers for his good friend's health who is currently in hospital fighting for his life' tagging dad in it, that the news broke and we could stay silent no more. Though it was meant well, it was very invasive and we weren't ready to deal with the bombardment of messages and phone calls that followed, and dad wasn't ready for everyone in his life to know. It was a desperate race against time to call important and close family and friends to tell them the news personally so that they wouldn't find out through Facebook.

When dad died, after we had made the same round of phone calls, my brother posted a status on Facebook informing the masses dad had passed and that funeral details would follow shortly. In this respect, social media was a great tool to disseminate the news with little effort on our part, meaning we could then answer the phone only when we wished and to who we wished, and could reply or 'like' messages as and when we felt like it. My brother's post received tons of likes, shares and comments, and people flocked to dad's Facebook page to post their messages of condolences there too. The response was overwhelming but in a good way. It was very surreal but very comforting to read the hundreds of messages written to dad and about dad from family, friends old and new, and people he had worked with over the years.

138

A funny and unexpected turn of events following dad's death was that he went viral…literally dad was trending. I don't really know how it started but various Hollywood magazines such as Hollywood Reporter, Deadline (the irony), and other platforms and fan pages like SPNHunters had publicised his death.

Four hours after dad died, Jim Beaver of *Supernatural* (Bobby), took to Twitter to share the news and his condolences. His tweet received 6,599 likes, 955 retweets and 205 comments…mind-blown! I remember sitting in an armchair in the apartment a couple of days later reading through all the comments totally in awe by the outpouring of comments from hundreds of people I will never know. It was extremely surreal to see strangers 'sending love and support to Cyrus's family', who I realised was me. You always see and hear such statements after a death or tragic event, but you never really expect to be the subject they are in reference to. There were some hardcore *24* and *Supernatural* fans who really pushed the boat out with their comments and posts on various fan cult pages. There was much frenzied, almost excited talk, about the fact dad died nine years to the day one of the most favoured directors of *Supernatural* had died.

Dad also got mentions in the Oscars and Emmy In Memorium segment on their respective websites. A warming nod that dad would have been pleased to have received, and in truth, something I had wondered in previous years whether dad would be a part of it when he dies.

Eerily dad also received a posthumous Wikipedia page, honestly no idea who created it or where they found the information stated on the page unless it was a family member's doing. Something that I find unsettling is that now if I Google dad, the first page is all about his death.

The first time I discovered this was a shock, I was trying to show somebody something and had to Google dad to find it, only to be met with a selection of obituaries and news of his passing. I lost my breath for a few moments as though a door had been slammed in my face and I could feel the whoosh of air fly past me. Something else that happened was that for nearly a year if I Googled my own name, (not something I do often), the random LinkedIn, Facebook or Instagram links had been replaced with the same search results as dad. It was as though dad's death, the very notion of it, had consumed our identity.

My heart still stops for a second when I scroll through my Facebook newsfeed and am met with someone posting a picture of themselves with dad declaring how much they miss him or recounting a funny story. Again, it's a weird juxtaposition between being heartfelt and warming to see, and being intrusive and catching me off-guard and emotionally unprepared to see it. I can never look for long or too hard at the images, I have to keep scrolling or quickly close the page.

LASTS AND FIRSTS

Is Time Even Linear?

One of my greatest cognitive struggles that I found it very hard to

rationalise and get my head around was the concept of time. For example, the dragging of time in each day, the hours spent sitting in hospital rooms and then getting into bed at the end of the day knowing I'd be doing it all over again tomorrow whilst lying in bed wondering how I'd managed to spend 10 or so hours in the room and not gone mad. By the time we'd get home from the hospital around seven or eight in the evening I'd slump into the armchair from which I could see the digital time on the DVD player and watch the minutes slowly go by until I could go to bed around nine and force myself asleep.

As a basic distraction I started doing crosswords on my phone, this made the time pass, maybe 20 to 30 minutes, depending on how hard it was and more often than not sent me to sleep. I did this every single night pretty much from the week following dad's passing and I still do it to this day. The hardest part of all to rationalise though was the passing of days to weeks and weeks to months, and months to a full year. I felt that my headspace was firmly stuck in November (learning the diagnosis), December and January (dealing with hospitals and dad's eventual death) and February (the month spent in LA encompassing the funeral and packing up dad's apartment). I cannot recall what I particularly did in March, April or May of that year. I had my big end of first year PhD exam in June so that's when I started to get more of a hold on time again. Even during those months I couldn't believe for example that whilst in May, April had been and gone, and that I'd been home from Los Angeles for three months by the time May 22nd had come around. The feeling of seeing Christmas decorations and merchandise gracing the aisles of shops and TV adverts from autumn felt overwhelming. Where had the months gone? Where had the year gone in fact? For me, time hadn't moved on. I started to wonder, is time even linear? Or is it related to memory?

Our family house in the Cotswolds where I grew up sits at the bottom of a hill surrounded by fields. From the window of my brother's bedroom you can see the road snake its way up and through the fields. Whenever dad was home from LA and had gone on a walk I'd run up to the window every ten minutes or so to see if he was on his way back down yet, sadness if not and a pang of excitement if he was. Even if he was at the very top of the view I'd set about either finishing what I was doing, shouting to mum that dad's nearly back, or kneel up on the bed and watch him walk down towards the house, banging on the window as he drew nearer.

I went home recently and found myself staring out of the window, I didn't realise what I was doing at first but I knew I wasn't just looking, I was *looking for something, someone.* I saw dad walking down the road, as clear as he always was. Slightly loose black jeans met bright white sneakers which really made him stand out against the grey tarmac and green hedgerows (and a giveaway that he was American), paired with a large black leather sports jacket and a black hat with a thick black fleeced rim. I could have been any age standing at the window, I will always see him walking down the hill towards me and always feel the excitement. So then, is time not cyclical?

Giving into the academic pull of the discipline I have been learning since 2011 I shall 'go all anthropology' on you for a bit here, but bear with me, I promise my musings will make sense. Sociologist Emile Durkheim posed that time is a fundamental aspect of human thought in his seminal book *The Elementary Forms of Religious Life* which he wrote in 1912. He contends that time is a 'collective representation' – something that on its own does not make sense, but in a social context or in a context in which a meaning is imbued upon something, time reflects our take on the reality that surrounds us. So, our lives don't just passively reflect time, we create time. As a result, the theory of temporal cultural relativism was developed which argues different cultures and societies interact and negotiate their lives in relation to time differently.

In addition, anthropologist Edmund Leach produced a theory asserting time encompasses two basic aspects of human life: firstly that certain things repeat themselves, for example earth orbits the sun, the moon comes out at night, some flowers bloom in spring, leaves fall off trees in autumn, your birthday comes around every year and so on; and secondly, that life change is irreversible. The first, a description of cyclical time, and the latter, indicative of linear time.

In my respect, dad dying is an irreversible life change, something that has happened and cannot be undone and therefore I must keep on going and not look back at what I cannot change. Another argument for time being linear is that we can know the past, we can't know the future. I can't know how I will feel in two years' time, or how much of my parents my children may have in their appearance or personality - thoughts which could offer comfort to my present.

With regard to death and mourning can the way we celebrate Christmas or now, the anniversary of dad's death, be seen as cyclical time in a ritualised sense? Does that mean then that linear time, the time passing between dad being alive or not, the irreversible reality, is more realistic and logical? Yet I experienced November 2017, December 2017, January 2018 and February 2018 in November and December of 2018 and January and February 2019. Of course not in real sense, but it was *real* in my mind, everyday of the previous year played out in my head as I met them from waking. In this sense perhaps linear and cyclical time have merged as cognitive trauma actors have manipulated the notion of time for me. Because linear time is seen to be objectively real (it is my 'outward' facing time), it dominates cyclical time that plays out in my head as the two attempt to coexist within me.

It wasn't only in this sense that cyclical time and linear time converged together, I found my physical location, emotional state, and context of time had all began to drip influence into each other. I'll explain: after dad died I returned to London at the end of February and once back I found myself going through the motions of the immediate stages of grieving all over again, as if dad had died the day I landed.

I now had to adapt my London life to being without him, something I had started to do for the past four weeks about my life in relation to Los Angeles. Fast-forward to December 2018 when I had returned from Los Angeles again back to London for Christmas. Stepping off the plane and going through the motions of getting to my boyfriend's flat from the airport and stages of jetlag had began to remind me of the previous time I had done this, the first time I'd returned after dad had died. It wasn't until a few days later when riding the over-ground in Vauxhall that the weight of emotions hit me and hurtled me back into the exact headspace I had been in all those months ago. But it wasn't just the emotions, I could smell those memories, I could hear the conversations I had playing out in my head as if I was having them for the first time in that moment in real life. I felt as though I had been transported back in time.

Thinking about all of this, I began to see the connection between time and emotion, how we reflect on time passing, and the interaction of time from the past, into the present and how that structures our lives in the future. To help myself understand this I reflected upon my own feelings and either subsequent or consequent experiences - in other words, the temporality of emotions. For example, whenever I sat down to pen more of this book from the notes I had taken throughout the year I was in a stable headspace, I felt good and energised. On days where I had the energy and motivation to write but my overarching emotions were sadness and anger, I could not write. I wonder what the tone of this would have been if I only wrote when I was in midst of crying fits and bouts of rage and resentment.

I then began to question customs and beliefs associated with grief and mourning and quickly came to the conclusion that emotion is a social construction operating on social and cultural levels. The temporal aspect of emotion is also reflexive of history and time-specific societal norms in the past. An example of how culture and society shape the norms of emotions in certain situations can be seen with Jews and their custom of 'sitting shiva', a seven-day culturally and religiously assigned formal mourning period. In this case, culture shapes emotion and the social context in which emotion is outwardly displayed.

I vividly remember learning about the Gitano Jarana people who actively forget the dead by reading the work of anthropologist Dr. Paloma Gay y Blasco. Her work explains that members of the community refrain from talking about the deceased or doing anything that might make others think of them either, for that is too painful. Possessions were burnt and photographs showing the deceased were either burnt or hidden, action must be taken to prevent the deceased from visiting the mind of the living. Because they love so deeply the pain of remembering or seeing the dead is too great. In contrast for example, research concerning death in Japan strongly highlights the importance of death and the afterlife in Japanese culture, such as commemorating the dead for decades through daily or monthly remembrance activities.

In our society we are taught to subdue our emotions in fear of upsetting the social order or those around us. We aren't accustomed to public wailing and cringe at PDAs. Is it that in Britain we are a bit 'embarrassed' by grief and have lost mourning rituals along the way? The Victorian era was potentially the last time Britain revelled in mourning customs following Queen Victoria's example - she was totally grief-stricken yet luxuriated in the mourning process following Prince Albert's death. Women became the embodiment of grief, wearing black mourning dress for a customary minimum of two years, families would pose with the deceased for a portrait or photograph, mirrors were covered in black fabrics, and nearly a year's seclusion from fun things was the custom.

In time perhaps these traditions were lost as a result of two World Wars seeing society cripple under mass mourning and public sentiment focused on survival rather than loss; the lyrics of a World War One marching song *'pack up your troubles in your old kit bag, and smile, smile, smile'* encourage stoicism. Sometimes I wished that we still had to wear head-to-toe black and a black veil when we are bereaved so people around me would know what I was going through, perhaps offer me a tissue or words of support on the tube rather than presumably assuming I was crying from a bad day at work or a breakup, or remorse tears over buying a house being pushed back another year because I'd been so reckless as to order avocado on toast for lunch.

We don't know what to say or how to act or what to eat or how to dress unlike some cultures who mourn as a community, but where does that leave other cultures today? The internet can operate as a mass community, forming lifelines for bereaved people who have no one in person to talk to, or perhaps want to talk behind the barrier of a keyboard, today people can also do social media mourning. Many people feel compelled to rush back to work for the distraction, or in fear of being let go or not wanting to seem like we're making a fuss or not helping ourselves by wallowing.

I thought about how much for me that grief is socially constructed and considered the juxtaposition between what we see when someone on TV dies and thus how we think we're meant to act (because we're not really taught about bereavement and death in mainstream education), as opposed to the reality of how we do act.

For example, I've had random laughter bouts in the most inappropriate times, such as telling someone dad had died, or in our initial meeting with the funeral director. Other bereaved people have told me similar stories such as laughing at the funeral or a fit of hysterics on the day their parent has died. It's not because we're evil and don't care, it's because our emotions are so skewed and all over the place our body is trying to figure out in what way to outwardly manifest them. In times of high anxiety laughter is a way that emotion is expelled from the body, and because this often occurs at inappropriate times, we become more anxious and thus the laughter becomes more intense. I wonder whether *Casualty* or *Grey's Anatomy* ever showed a family who have just learned of a loved one passing rolling around on the floor in hysterics rather than in floods of tears.

Emotions are a response to action and thought. I've mourned deeply because dad had a deep meaning for me. Our personal emotions are unique to the way we perceive and experience reality, yet are situated in our past (built upon previous experiences), our present, and our future (planning what may lie ahead, or taking action so as to cause or prevent something). As a result, it can be argued that the temporality of our emotions is cyclical as reflecting on emotions imbued with meaning allows us to move backward and forward temporally. Past thoughts and experiences can be cognitively and emotionally reconstructed through memory with intense emotion seeming to stop or slow time.

The meaning of emotion in the present is built upon the meaning I have given to the past, not just the traumatic experiences of dad being ill, but the meaning I assigned to my relationship with dad throughout my life. So emotions that are linked to my past influence how I enact present behaviour, which is why my present and future is affected by my past more than when I learn about a death of a stranger on the news.

149

In a previous chapter I have explained how my grief has changed and evolved as a result of passage of time as well as the feelings I have towards my identity, both inwardly and my outward appearance, for example, my reflection and a perceived loss of 'innocence'. If anything has been a rite of passage to becoming an adult is has definitely been caring for my dad and witnessing his death.

An interesting yet probably quite depressing investigation would be of collective representations of time, or in other words how time is created and experienced, by a mass group of bereaved individuals. I feel this would not only shine light on cognitive notions of time whilst grieving, but also physical and biological. For example, no matter how hard I might try to block a date out of my head like dad's birthday or his death anniversary, my body knows. My body knows on the day of, and my body knows in the days leading up to it, and I'm left anxious, nauseous, exhausted, dazed and aching. I would like to consider more deeply the temporality of emotions during mourning periods and beyond, setting grief against the continuum of time.

Memorial Park

Being someone who would prefer to be cremated than buried, I never considered myself to be someone who would visit an interred person. Before I experienced dad's death I thought that the person would live on in my mind and I would visit them there and the place of burial an abstract and symbolic entity.

Once dad died this assumption was turned on its head. In Jewish tradition there is an unveiling ceremony 11 months after the death in which the headstone is unveiled and various prayers recited. As mum, my brother and I are not Jewish we adapted this tradition to suit our beliefs. We did this in September so did not wait out the customary 11 months and we unveiled the headstone by closing our eyes on our approach and opening them once in front, in a 'ta-dah' kind of fashion. In dad's case, the headstone was a large granite plaque placed upon his area of the wall crypt but it had private conversations with him rather than prayers. We had requested 'yippeekadoodles' to be written on his plaque, a word dad implored at every joyful or proud moment, and the engravings of an olive branch between his dates and a tree of life on each side, like a border.

For some reason I dressed up for the event, I guess it just felt right and I wanted to look nice for dad who I hadn't seen in a while. I selected a short-sleeved tomato-red top (a quick Google told me red wasn't an overtly symbolically offensive colour in Judaism), which I paired with gold metallic trousers and matching red heeled sandals. I knew dad would really like the outfit. We also took photos of the plaque to send to family and friends, with a few of us standing beside it.

Bearing in mind he's on the 'sixth floor' I had to teach mum some quick camera angle tips to make sure it wasn't just a picture of the plaque and my forehead upwards, but instead (obviously) my whole outfit, shoes included because the open-toe style of them revealed that my toenails were in fact the same turquoise colour of my earrings…it's all in the detail. This was kind of weird, a bit like taking a photo at a tourist attraction, but dad loved taking photographs so it was still in line with his personality.

My brother drove us to the memorial park, the first time we'd been back since the funeral. As we approached the entrance the gateman came out requesting our business, and all three of us mumbled and jumbled out the words along the lines of 'we're here to visit our dad/husband'. It felt very odd. We parked as close as we could to where the wall crypts were and walked over.

The memorial park is beautiful and the walk from the nearest road includes grass, private but open-air burial sections for families, murals, benches, tropical flowers and water fountains. The park had a way of calming my atmosphere as if someone had thrown a thin chiffon scarf over me, and as I walked across to the wall crypt I thought to myself that this will be a walk that, for as long as I continue to visit, will be a constant in my life. My dad will always be there and so I will always be treading this route. It was a hard thought to understand and I don't know if it made me feel anxious, or settled and comforted in some way,. It was just weird suddenly having an absolute concrete place for the rest of my life.

Once in front of dad's wall crypt I found it hard to look up and then once my eyes had found him, hard to look away. I naively thought I'd be fine visiting, having predetermined in my mind that 'it won't mean anything' and 'dad's not really in there' to actually finding myself really struggling with the fact dad was very much in there. No matter how hard I tried I couldn't separate the idea of dad being in the wall to the notion of dad being alive and this thought made me feel sick to my stomach and very claustrophobic. I couldn't separate his body from his soul - and his presence that people keep telling me is now all around me - not in the wall. I felt as though a veil of sadness had been draped over me, I didn't cry but I did feel anger and I felt a lot of guilt whenever I thought about leaving. The first real sensation of guilt since dad had died. I didn't really know what I should or should not have thought about whilst there. Did my thoughts have to be purely about dad, was it wrong for my mind to wonder back to focusing on what was going on in my current life.

The second time I visited dad was the day before I was due to fly back to London for Christmas. I felt very strongly that it was something I had to do, I had to say Merry Christmas and let him know I was going and give a more 'in-person' update of what I'd been up to. I was worried that if I didn't go, I'd fly out of LAX and over the city and be hit with a pang of anxiety that I hadn't visited. What if somehow he was waiting for me there to say Merry Christmas and I never showed up? It was strange going by myself, honestly I thought I'd find it a bit eerie but the warm winter sun was beating down and the birds were still singing and again I felt an overarching sense of calm as I walked through the memorial park having got dropped off at the gates in an Uber.

How I felt in sum is a actually a hard sensation to explain. This time I was overcome with emotion and cried hard, perhaps being by myself enabled me to do this, and at the same time I felt a really overwhelming sense of anger, anger at how unfair everything had turned out for us. Unfair for dad, unfair for me, unfair for my mum and brother and other family members. The best way to describe it is by imagining I am a little statue inside of a snow-globe that has just been violently shaken. All the snow flakes whizzing around me are anger, resentment and sadness, yet the glass container curved over me is the peace and calmness that stepping into the memorial park seemed to exude.

I had an internal monologue of how long I should stay, what was an appropriate length of time? Was that thought offensive in itself? That I was thinking what's the minimum amount of time acceptable to stay without seeming disrespectful or as though I didn't care? What should I do? Was it rude to lean on the wall…might I accidentally knock something and the wall open revealing a stranger's casket within? I fought hard to suppress such thoughts. In the end the monologue was a waste of mental energy as I ended up staying for about an hour, acknowledging my grief, updating dad, and then taking in the surroundings.

In the memorial park across the fence, the (non-Jewish) cemetery, I could see a service taking place that was being accompanied by a mariachi band which I found quite cheering and decided to quietly play dad some of his favourite songs from my phone. I was sure his neighbours wouldn't have

154

minded some *Buena Vista Social Club* of Dean Martin's *Amore*. I turned my phone down a bit more when I put Spike Jones' *Cocktails For Two* on although I was sure it would liven things up a bit, excuse the pun. I laughed along at the songs with tears in my eyes, still bitterly feeling the unfairness that dad couldn't enjoy the songs in the way I wanted him to.

I decided it was time to leave when the sun had started to set, knowing I had about a 20-minute walk through the park to the gates. Being in the mountains there were also a lot of signs warning visitors of snakes, deer, mountain lions and coyotes which I was definitely hoping to avoid a dusk encounter with. Like before, I felt a lot of guilt leaving. The thought of leaving him behind, in the wall, still felt so wrong. I found myself internally almost apologising to him that he couldn't fly back to England with me and assuring him I'd come back and say hello as soon as I was back in Los Angeles in the spring.

Christmas

Christmas 2017 was a strange one for several reasons. I'd spent the last few weeks being sad that we wouldn't be back in England for Christmas to celebrate with family as we usually do, as well as grappling with the thought that dad would never be in England again.

Dad loved coming home to the Cotswolds, which he always did over the Christmas period, and if he could, a few times throughout the year too. Dad was a school-gate favourite amongst the parents and my primary school comrades and his half New York, half Californian accent would ring out loud and clear through the village on our walk home. Something I found deeply embarrassing, because at that age, I found everything deeply embarrassing.

Dad was also a member of the village golf club, although only partook in the Christmas tournament and always came last. We'd say, *'don't let us down, got to keep up your track record'* and off he'd go, returning at the end of the day, fist pumping the air above him saying, *'I came last!'*, to which mum, my brother and I would all join in with the cheering and pour a glass of merlot.

It wasn't until a week or so before the 25th that dad finally stopped asking when we'd be going or holding onto hope that he'd be well enough to fly. After he stopped asking we never discussed the fact of spending Christmas in Los Angeles, he fell silent on the issue of country and started his campaign to be home from the hospital in time. As a result I spent the run-up to Christmas dreading the day and not wanting to celebrate it at all. It felt wrong but it also felt too sad.

Selfishly I missed the festive activities I'd usually partake in back in England like ice-skating, Winter Wonderland in Hyde Park, seeing *The Nutcracker*, lots of drinking and parties and watching Christmas films like *Elf* with hot chocolate and cheese and crackers. I particularly missed an advent calendar; I couldn't find one anywhere. It was hard to feel festive with everything going on with dad but also being in sunny Los Angeles. Despite the trees being adorned with lights and speakers blaring out Christmas songs, 'It's beginning to look a lot like Christmas' and 'Let it snow, let it snow, let it snow' sounded very out of place.

We made the very last-minute decision to still have a 'proper' Christmas food wise and so I set about on Christmas Eve with mum in Whole Foods finding a turkey while my brother stayed home with dad who had managed to get out of hospital for a few days. I don't remember much of Christmas Eve other than mum's joy at being able to find the clip on Radio 4 of this year's *Once in Royal David's City from* 'Carols from King's' and at dusk walking a few blocks to where a model of Santa in his sleigh, laden with presents and with all the reindeer, had been strung across a vast intersection. I guess I did it for a semblance of Christmas cheer. We hadn't sung any carols that year and the only Christmas trees I'd seen were the oversized ones in the hospital and one at the airport decorated in American Airlines merchandise.

157

I went to sleep letting myself dwell on happier years where we'd set down a glass of sherry and mince pie for Father Christmas and a carrot for Rudolph by the front door before going to bed, and then pretending to be asleep as mum and dad filled my little stocking that hung on my door with chocolates and placed a present at the end of my bed. We were always allowed to open one present when we woke up, but would then wait until the rest of the family arrived before opening others.

I woke on Christmas morning feeling slightly lighter than the day before, perhaps I'd resigned to the day and tried to make the most of it. I got up and made dad some breakfast and sorted out all his medication for the day. We'd normally all sit around the kitchen table showing off our opened presents and quickly tucking into a *pain-au-chocolat* before tending to the turkey and driving it round to our grandma's house down the road whose oven it would cook in for four hours. Our oven would be full of vegetables, roasties and chipolatas.

I picked out a pretty navy woollen dress to wear and did my makeup fully and curled my hair a bit. I wanted to make an effort and look nice, as well as it being a coping mechanism against crying. I tried to act normal, even getting dad to take some pictures of me and a boomerang of me drinking champagne, (circa 10am, it was needed) and chastising him when they turned out blurry.

Once mum and my brother were dressed too we set up a self-timer and took some photos of the four of us. All feigning a smile, pretending to be happy and it not being weird. I feel odd looking at these photos now,

158

they're the last photos we have of dad out of hospital and dressed in normal clothes, but he looks so ill and there's so much pain within all of our eyes.

Christmas dinner wasn't the same and dad wasn't able to eat much of it due to his harsh dietary restrictions and lack of appetite. We munched on treats sent over from our English family and spent the afternoon watching films, *The Shape of Water* and *I, Tonya* before going for a brief walk up and down the road, as much as dad could manage with his arms around myself and my brother, either side, helping him along but he napped for a lot of the day.

Boxing Day didn't seem to be an event in America and so rather than our usual roast beef and walks, we had an important doctor's meeting. The 'big' one, the one where we'd see if there was anything else we could do. I replied to various messages from people back home sending me pictures of their Boxing Day meals, or cosy scenes at their fireplaces with my sad wilted salad from the hospital canteen.

The appointment went 'well'. We were told there was an experimental drug dad could try but first we'd have to check to see if it was covered by dad's medical insurance. Everything came down to money and insurance. An intravenous drug called Rituxan which would help with the lymphoma. But there was still the issue of the lung cancer and the cancer that had spread to his bones, and his kidneys, which were now reliant on dialysis every other day. The doctor said dad had at least another six months. When we returned to the apartment mum and dad

159

encouraged me to book a flight back to England for some normality. Little did we know then that the doctor's six-month prediction was off by five months.

Although in England, I also faced Christmas 2018 with dread and apprehension about the day and was already emotionally and mentally exhausted from thinking about it by the time Christmas Eve came around. Everything was different, starting with the structure of the day and a change in family roles and responsibilities. I helped mum with the tasks that dad always did on Christmas morning like washing, prepping and stuffing the turkey, and getting the extra chairs down from the loft and rearranging the living room furniture to get the kitchen table next to the dining table.

It wasn't that I couldn't be bothered to do these tasks, but they felt wrong and to all of us an emphasis that dad was missing. Once other family members arrived and presents had started to be unwrapped the role of collecting the wrapping paper in a bin bag as it was strewn around the room needed a new leader - traditionally dad's role - as well as new delegates to drive round to grandma's every hour or so to baste the turkey.

I managed to get through most of the day by alternating between pretending it wasn't Christmas and that dad was simply held up at work and couldn't make it, like so many people who have to work on Christmas Day. This illusion only held until about 5pm when reality shattered the cracks in my daydream, exposing the harsh truth that dad was gone, the space at the table wouldn't be filled, there were no Christmas presents to or from dad this year.

Up until this point I'd felt dad was like the elephant in the room, no one had really mentioned he wasn't here, I supposed, so as not to upset anyone, but as the day went on it felt wrong, like we were all complicit in actively forgetting or erasing him. My eyes couldn't hold back the tears that had been lying in wait behind the surface any longer and my floodgates opened. By seeing various family members cracking too we all realised dad wouldn't want us to be sad, but he certainly wouldn't want us to forget him. We started to share stories of dad which although sad made the evening a lot cosier and warmer. Statements such as *'this was Cyrus' favourite'* or *'Cyrus loved this wine'*, *'he really enjoyed this'* or *'remember that Christmas when dad did….'* started to be shared around and my uncle, who was in charge (with dad) of what we called the 'bonhomie' began to laugh more and the classic and dire dad-jokes began to seep their way back into conversation.

New Year's

New Year's Eve 2017 into 2018 went much the same as Christmas. I don't remember what we did during the day for New Year's Eve but I remember the evening being a particularly dire and morbid affair, despite our best efforts for it not to be.

Dad was still home from the hospital, albeit very tired and weak so we spent a lot of the day on the sofa watching the rest of the world bring in the New Year. Los Angeles is one of the last time zones to cross over so it was strange getting midnight messages from friends back home when it was only 4pm for us. Dad, mum and I were all sat on the sofa, in that order, I physically couldn't sit in the middle despite my mum encouraging me to do so. I couldn't face it, I couldn't face sitting through the evening next to dad, wondering how many more times I'd be able to snuggle up to him, and at the same time couldn't face resting my cheek on his shoulder feeling how bony he'd become or risk causing him pain. It seems like an awful missed opportunity now, but I literally just couldn't do it.

I remember we made the terrible mistake of watching *Three Billboards Outside Ebbing, Missouri.* Though a good film overall we couldn't escape the montage of scenes of the sheriff finding out he had cancer, penning a long and detailed account of why he doesn't want to deteriorate and die in front of his wife and children before taking himself out into the yard and shooting himself. We sat there is absolute silence, no one looked at each other, the cringe levels in the room were palpable.

Why is it that any mention of death or someone dying causes people to feel flushed and hot, avoid eye contact at all costs and feel their toes curling up? *Finally*, and seriously it felt like a very long time coming, Los Angeles welcomed the New Year. We watched the fireworks, dad faintly muttered *l'chaim* ('to life…'), we cheers-ed and hurried around to get to bed by which point it was already 8am in England. We were never really a family that did much on New Year's Eve or New Year's Day. The year before in fact the four of us had spent it in the living room of our house in England with my mum and I lying on sofas with blankets over us and buckets by our heads having succumbed to the norovirus and dad pottering nervously between us with fresh water and tissues. Nothing felt 'happy' about this 'Happy New Year'.

On New Year's Day mum and I went for lunch with a close family friend round the corner from dad's apartment. He woke up not feeling well enough to have visitors in the apartment nor the energy to walk to the café so we left him with my brother. Mum and I eagerly ordered large glasses of wine and although anxious about what may be happening in the flat, revelling in our chance to be outside. By the time lunch was over and we'd returned to the apartment dad was in such a way that we needed to take him back into hospital, and thus began our 2018.

I spent New Year's Eve 2018 into 2019 in Inverness in Scotland with my boyfriend at his family home. So 2019 was brought in with Hogmanay celebrations, champagne and party poppers and being bumped and hurled into random people like dodgems, which I thought was a pretty ironic metaphor of how I'd spent the past year feeling. If you haven't guessed yet, I was at a ceilidh. Not really being New Year's kind of people, I knew mum wouldn't mind that I was spending it elsewhere, and partaking in my first Hogmanay was actually really fun.

The day before New Year's Eve, however, I felt the creeping anxiety slowly bubble and begin to consume me again, the now-familiar feeling of when 'something' was about to happen without dad. There were lots of distractions on New Year's Eve Day, more of my boyfriend's family arriving, a couple of hours at a bowling alley, lasagne, new nail polish to go with my outfit, a few YouTube makeup tutorials and the process of getting ready for a night out, something I often enjoyed more than the night out itself. By 9pm six of us had set off to the barn where the New Year's ceilidh was being held. A happy coincidence it was in the neighbouring barn because walking in a dress and heels in the dead of winter in the Scottish Highlands was definitely not ideal.

I had managed to suppress my growing sadness and anxiety for most of the day until at the entrance to the farm I saw a handmade sign showing we were in the right place and to keep walking to the top of the long farm track to the barn to reach the festivities. It was the sign that threw me off the imaginary perfectly balanced emotional ledge I had positioned myself on. It was the sign that made me think, 'what am I doing?', 'how can I be going out and having fun?', I felt physically sick to my stomach and felt my face drop as goose bumps took over my body. But there was no turning back, I wasn't going to let my emotions get in the way of others having fun, and instead focused on not drawing attention to myself which would only have been a downer for everyone else.

164

I remember it being mentally so difficult to push the feeling out of my body, as if I was pushing a huge boulder, but I had to do it, and dad would have wanted me to have a good time. I decided not to drink too much for fear of getting too drunk and emotional and I did end up having a really great time, it wasn't until the walk back, which also included rain, that I started feeling anxious and sick again.

Once back at the house, my boyfriend, his siblings, other plus-ones and I gathered around the kitchen table for a debrief of the night, and jealous of their seemingly care-free joviality, I consoled myself by attacking the cheese and cold meats in the fridge, presumably intended for New Year's Day.

Then New Year's Day happened – and it was awful. Quite possibly one of the worst days I had experienced since dad died. I felt incredibly tired, defeated, crushed, low, numb. If I were a colour I would have been grey, a bland, dark, ominous grey. Social media was overwhelming, so many people sharing statements of how amazing their year had been, or their favourite photos from 2018, wishing everyone a beautiful 2019 with smug smiling faces. I flicked through Facebook and Instagram in disgust as each post tore me apart a bit more - I made myself stop in the end and didn't allow myself back on for a couple of days.

I know I was being overly critical and cynical as people only show the best bits of their lives and are probably miserable about something as well, but I just didn't want to see anything about 'what a great year 2018 was!'. I shied away from all sayings such as '2018 was a great year' or worse, '2018 was a good year, apart from a couple of bumps', or 'let's hope for a better 2019' which felt like a knife to the stomach each time. I thought, how could 2019 be better? At least dad was in 2018, even for a little bit. How can any year then be better than 2018?

I actually hadn't really anticipated feeling this way on New Year's Day, and was shocked that I felt drastically worse than I had done over Christmas. It was the fear and anxiety that was so destabilising and debilitating, the guilt and confusion of no longer being in 2018, leaving behind 2018, leaving behind the trauma of 2018, and leaving behind dad. To me, it felt like he was stuck there as we got to go on with our lives and crossed over into a New Year. It was almost as though this meant he could now be swept under the rug and forgotten about…dad died *last year*. It felt unbelievably wrong.

Yahrzeit

Thursday 24th January 2019, the day before the one-year anniversary, I woke up with a duvet of apprehension over me. Even out of bed the layer had not been stripped away. I knew tomorrow was approaching but I couldn't really explain how I felt other than anxious and stressed. I felt all day that I needed to do something, like I was very restless. It wasn't until later in the afternoon that I realised why this was probably the case.

The day before dad passed was for me the more stress inducing and adrenaline fuelled day than the day dad actually died. This was the day I'd received the phone call to get on the next flight and then endured 12 hours flying across the globe not knowing if I'd make it in time, then rushing to the hospital and first laying my eyes on the deteriorated state cancer had forced upon dad's appearance.

I found myself grieving for myself, replaying my day in my head and pitying myself as my cousins helped me numbly throw clothes into my suitcase and dashed through the airport as if I was watching this scene play out in a movie. I also grieved for dad, a sick twisting in my stomach feeling thinking about whether in those last hours he felt pain or panic or intense sadness. I wondered whether he could feel any emotion at all or whether by that time the cancer had robbed him of all senses and cognitive ability other than maybe his hearing, I wondered whether this was a good or bad thing.

It was also during this time that images of dad before his diagnosis pushed their way into my head. They felt almost like an intrusion, it was nice to see his smiling or laughing face looking at me, but I wasn't ready. It made me too sad, it made me angry at the universe that this vibrant man had been robbed of ever smiling again.

I spent most of the day doing work on the sofa and pottering around the flat cleaning and cooking, anything to distract myself from my thoughts. By 9pm I felt I was suffocating, I got in the shower and belted out 'On My Own' from *Les Mis* on repeat for the duration of the shower. I know this is a bit macabre but sometimes where you're feeling sorry for yourself the only way to release the emotion is to ride it out and really indulge in it. I quickly transported myself into different hypothetical scenarios where I was singing this song, myself as Eponine on the West End, or being at a karaoke bar with friends and having this song come up as it was my turn to take the mic. I was particularly encouraged by how I got into the facial expressions during different lyrics. 'The river's *just* a river' was a line I spat out with meticulous rage and fat hot tears running down my face splashing into the water building up in the bath around my feet.

I changed genre for my post-shower drying and walking-to-bedroom accompaniment, Sia and David Guetta's 'Flames', a good motivational song whilst still allowing you to revel in self-pity but upbeat enough to help you get through the tears faster. Once dressed I slumped onto the sofa and cried to my boyfriend. We made cups of tea and debated whether something sweet to eat would make me feel better before finding a comedy to watch on Netflix.

25th January 2019. The day of. I woke up feeling strange, I didn't know how I felt at that moment and I didn't know how I was *supposed* to feel, in the same way I didn't know how to feel the year before. I disliked when people asked me what I was planning on doing on this day and suggest I take some time to think about him and some memories. Though I found this sentiment irritating, I realised that people who hadn't lost someone close to them were suggesting this.

They didn't know that when death strikes, in the beginning you think about that person *all* the time, I didn't need to take some time today to think about dad, I thought about him permanently. I didn't linger in bed for long but instead got up and showered and tea-ed and breakfasted. We'd bought a Just-Rol pack of pain-au-chocolat and experimented with different flavours like adding cinnamon and chopped pear. This was good distraction for about an hour, I then booked a last-minute hair appointment for the following hour. I thought that as long as I can keep myself busy I'll be fine. In a way I felt as though I'd released all of my emotions the evening before, I did actually feel better.

It was a 20 or so minute walk to the hairdresser's but I left early so as not to linger and risk getting upset, which meant I arrived early at my appointment. I sat in the hairdresser's chair making idle small-talk with those around me and explaining how I wanted my hair cut.

I looked in the mirror: why is it that you're at your ugliest at a hair salon? No one looks good in those mirrors, the bright white lights made my skin sallow and pale and enhanced the deep purple bags and my eyes and the blue veins popping out of my skin, my head and neck framed with a heavy plastic wrap placed over my shoulders.

It's as though the mirrors have the Clarendon Instagram filter built into them. Staring past my reflection, my eyes wandered around the room to everyone else. Didn't they know my dad died a year ago today? It's like when it's your birthday and you're sat on the tube and you look around the carriage and find it strange that today's an important day for you, but nobody around you has the faintest idea.

I asked for the massage chair to be turned on whilst my hair was being washed. My favourite part is always the head massage you get during what I presume is in the waiting-for-the-conditioner-to-work phase of a hair wash. 'Killed two birds with one stone', I thought, a bit of pampering in the form of a new haircut and a massage.

As I was walking home I confessed to myself that a bit of interaction with other humans and mindlessly thumbing through the pages of *OK!* and *Hello!* magazine (a hair salon guilty pleasure) had cheered me up in a sense of transporting me from being inside my head and dwelling on the day, to having to talk about mundane and normal-life things. This thought cheered me up until I came to a set of traffic lights. I stood waiting for the lights to change and looked over the road where my eyes met five men, likely in their 20s and wearing clothing that suggested they were possibly builders all looking back at me and shouting across the road trying to get my attention. Their comments were variations of '*hello*', '*hi*' and *'how are you'* which was met with an intense resting-bitch-face. I couldn't even be bothered to crack a smile. 'Not today', I thought. My silence and glares seemed to rile them up more and they started frantically waving at me and laughing amongst themselves. 'Seriously, are you 12?' was my next thought. It was exhausting to watch their childish behaviour. The light turned red and I crossed the road silently looking directly through them.

As the day progressed I continued to have an internal monologue with myself about how I should be feeling. I was comforted by various friends and family reaching out to me, sending well wishes and lots of heart emojis. I found myself analysing why certain people had reached out and certain people hadn't. I tried not to take offence at those who hadn't remembered, why would or should they? A classic case of no one else's world has stopped. I also noticed I had peaks and troughs to my day, some parts my emotions were closer to the surface and I enjoyed reading the messages I was receiving, but at other times when I was feeling OK, I found myself shying away from checking my phone.

My dad had a tradition that when someone died he would send a bottle of champagne to those who were grieving, and drink champagne himself as a toast to their life. At 6pm my boyfriend and I headed out to a cocktail bar and ordered a glass of champagne and lychee martinis. We 'cheered' and I smiled and felt that that was all I needed to do today as homage to dad, like when you buy someone a cake on their birthday. As time differences caught up I received messages and photos of other champagne corks being popped from the East to the West coast of

America. The thought of a global chain of champagne-drinking in celebration of dad's life made me smile, I knew he'd be laughing.

MY YEAR IN HINDSIGHT

So much has changed in the past year - the first year without dad. It

seems like there has just been so much going on, so many new things in my life and avenues I have gone down. Yet at the same time, it feels like no time has passed at all and it feels absurd to even think about how much has happened in the last 12 months. Absurd because dad wasn't part of it. How can it really be a year since we spoke on the phone?

I don't know whether the following are regrets as such, or more just self-pity, but I wish I had gone easier on myself and really realized and 'appreciated' the gravity of the situation. Allowed myself time to grieve, time to breath, time to wallow, time to lie in bed all day and watch films and cry, time to turn down social events and not feel guilty about doing so, time off.

My PhD supervisor warned me *'no one is super human'* and her words have stuck with me. In times of intense sadness and despair I replayed these words and allowed myself to take a deep breath and put aside my work for a while. Though I'm shocked at how well I was able to 'carry on' as normal, work wise, I knew it was a coping mechanism for me, giving me something to focus on. If I hadn't done what I have done such as carrying on with my studies I wouldn't be where I am today, and knowing my personality, this would have resulted in a worse mental toll.

In the same vein, I feel as though I am almost feeling the gravity of the situation now because I spent the first year in shock, denial and machine mode. I feel as though I am experiencing a sensation of double grieving. Grieving the loss of dad but now also for myself (my past self) and what I put myself through last year. But again, I am proud of myself for carrying on and achieving what I did but wish I hadn't been so hard on myself and so anxious of deadlines and whether I had done enough in a day.

I look back almost in shock at the things I did in the immediate weeks and few months following dad's death, things that now seem so ridiculous, like why did I put that pressure on myself and pretend that I was OK?! Why did I feel so, so guilty for cancelling plans or leaving early? I remember on the two-month mark of dad's passing feeling awful and guilty because I was (obviously) having a down day but hosting overnight guests, friends of my partner's who I hadn't met before. Though no one made me feel like this, I felt like I needed to suppress my emotions, which in hindsight is ridiculous because any sane person would appreciate that being remotely welcoming, active and energetic within two months of a parent's death is a hard task. I remember trying to make a good impression, gleefully cooking up a big pasta dish, robotically stirring the pot, my eyes completely glazed over as if they were looking inward at the memories of trauma replaying in my mind throughout.

I wish I wasn't so hard on myself for not wanting to be around people I didn't really know or large social settings. I felt very uncomfortable in such social situations where I didn't know who knew about dad and who didn't. For example, friends of friends, and therefore not knowing how to answer questions like 'how are you?', 'how have you been?', or knowing what to say when people say 'haven't seen you in a while', 'have you been in America?'. Saying, 'yeah I was in America because my dad died and so no I'm not really that great' seemed to abrupt and 'in your face'. I hated to think I was making anyone feel awkward by telling them the truth and then having to watch their cheeks flush beetroot, fumble around a little, look down and mumble a condolence. They obviously all would mean well but I didn't like putting them in that position and it wasn't any great shakes of a conversation to endure myself either.

Perhaps it comes with every age, but at 24/25 I felt immense pressure to still be going out, having fun and looking like I was having fun, having drinks and revelling in large social situations yet the more I made myself do it, actually the worse I felt. I felt like an outsider and 'the lame one', with each event making me draw further into myself, aware of how I must look to others and feeling whatever social kudos I had ebb away. Fear of now being Rose, who doesn't like to stay out late, or Rose, who won't drink a lot. Whether this is all in my head I'm not sure, but in hindsight, I wish I was kinder to myself in this respect. Similarly, it is OK for my life goals, ambitions, path and priorities to have changed. It is OK to now want different things to some of my friends who haven't experienced grief and can still seemingly be carefree in their day-to-day lives.

It is also important to talk to friends openly about how you're feeling and what support you need. Ask for help, admit when you're feeling rubbish, talk about mental health. This can be quite a daunting thought but at the end of the day, if they don't care or lose interest, then are they really friends? Though it has been painful to realize, some friends are no longer as close as we once were, or I still believed to be. It has also been a time of inward thought and reflection. I have found myself reevaluating friendships and relationships – thinking about what they have given me over the last year and how appreciative I am of that. Equally I have thought about the ways I would like certain friendships to progress and the positivity and support that I want to harbour with people. Honestly, there have been a lot of revisions to the hypothetical bridesmaid list!

When you're living with grief it is OK to want and do what makes you feel good, and as long as its not hurting anybody, you shouldn't care what other people may think about it. Say yes, say no, be selfish. Remember the wise words: what somebody thinks of you is none of your business.

One of the biggest feelings I have had since dad died is thinking 'but what is the point?' What is the point because dad won't be there to see it, know it, hear it, experience it. I still think this frequently and it is a hard thought to rise out from but I remind myself that by thinking this way I am forgetting everyone else who will be there to see it, hear it, experience it and support me and be proud of me.

Perhaps again this is an age thing, and like I said at the beginning of this book, at a time when I am somewhere in no-man's-land between independence and reliance on my parents. I am still learning and working on this and it has been a slow process with many setbacks and flailing arms whilst my body slumps into a chair, but I have begun to shift my focus from doing things with subliminal intent of gaining parental validation or thinking 'ooh won't my parents be happy or proud of me', to doing things for me. Doing things for my future, whether that's setting myself up a little bit better financially, professionally, or giving myself more stability (something I have been craving since receiving dad's diagnosis) or for when in the future I have my own family I can be the strong, brave female role model I had from my family growing up.

A key virtue to remember is patience. I always reiterate to myself the death of someone close to you and bereavement is like a physical wound.

Be patient with yourself, look after yourself, and listen to yourself. If you feel better one day, enjoy it, if you don't, then don't angst about it, know that you have to ride out the emotions. Importantly, allow yourself to rest in order to heal.

Yes, there's loneliness, but there's also something a bit powerful knowing that no one can feel what you are feeling right now. Ride the emotions out, feel the pain, feel the screams burn up inside you and career out of your mouth, find yourself on the floor, or in bed at 3pm, and grow from it, you got through it, you're coming out the other side.

Getting through each day is a process, sometimes a really difficult day and sometimes a lighter happier day. Once you acknowledge this, living with grief becomes just a little bit more manageable and you will grow more than you thought possible. It takes courage to grieve. You can do anything now, be brave, you're getting through this, you can push through other barriers. Your life might not be anywhere near 'perfect' now, but you can live your life with courage and bravery instead, and once you realize this, so many more doors will open in front of you.

Printed in Poland
by Amazon Fulfillment
Poland Sp. z o.o., Wrocław

49521710R00115